LYNCHBURG

A CITY SET ON SEVEN HILLS

Craddock and Terry office staff Fourth of July picnic, 1917. (Irma D. Pierson)

LYNCHBURG

A CITY SET ON SEVEN HILLS

CLIFTON POTTER AND
DOROTHY POTTER

ARCADIA
PUBLISHING

Published by Arcadia Publishing,
Charleston SC, Chicago IL, Portsmouth NH, San Francisco CA

Printed in the United States

Library of Congress control number: 2003115294

For all general information contact Arcadia Publishing at:
Telephone 843-853-2070
Fax 843-853-0044
E-Mail sales@arcadiapublishing.com
For customer service and orders:
Toll-Free 1-888-313-2665

Visit us on the Internet at www.arcadiapublishing.com

Bob & Ruthann Tile
@
Lynchburg Aug 2013

CONTENTS

ACKNOWLEDGMENTS

History seems to be part of the very air we breathe in Lynchburg. Everyone has an anecdote to share, a memory lovingly treasured and passed from one generation to another. To all of those persons, who were so generous with their time and their stories, we thank you.

Jones Memorial Library is a treasure trove of local history, and without access to its collections this book would have been impossible to write. Most of the photographs are copied from its vast archives. However, it is the staff of Jones that deserves special recognition. Head Librarian Wayne Rhodes, Lewis Averett, Nancy Weiland, and Susan Pillow were never too busy to answer each and every question, be it trivial or be it complicated.

Nancy Blackwell Marion of The Design Group generously shared her expertise and copied dozens of photographs from the electronic catalog she has compiled. The clarity of her prints from the Jones Memorial Library collection, as well as those from The *Lynchburg News*, brings precious and often fragile photographs back to life.

Carol Spencer Read, the daughter of Chauncey Spencer and the granddaughter of Edward and Anne Spencer, opened her family's archive and shared her valuable collection of photographs with us. Thus we were able to explore in detail the lives of two persons who helped to advance the positive process of transforming Lynchburg into a more inclusive community.

The staff at the Knight-Capron Library at Lynchburg College was always available to obtain works from other libraries, and to help us access the vast electronic resources accessible to modern scholars. Linda Carder, Elizabeth Henderson, and Ariel Myers deserve a special thank you. Two members of the Lynchburg College Department of Information Technology and Resources merit special mention. Wendall Russell lent his skills as a photographer, and Nathan Formo was particularly helpful in scanning the photographs and preparing the text for publishing using the latest technology.

A special thanks is due Jim Kempert and Rob Kangas of Arcadia Publishing, who answered every question quickly and completely. Their guidance in the preparation of this manuscript has been invaluable.

Acknowledgments

Edmund Potter, the Curator of Collections at the Woodrow Wilson Presidential Library at His Birthplace in Staunton, Virginia, lent valuable assistance in preparing the chapter on the two World Wars. His advice on the selection of photographs from that era also proved useful.

The *Lynchburg News*, the Academy of Fine Arts, and Randolph-Macon Woman's College generously gave us the opportunity to search their archives and reproduce photographs from their sizeable collections. The Southern Memorial Association, the Lynchburg Museum System, the Lynchburg Historic Foundation, Inc., and the Legacy Museum allowed us to examine their repositories for those random facts that hopefully give this history depth and breadth.

A special thank you is reserved for the Monacan Nation, and especially Chief Kenneth Branham. The welcome we received from members of this tribe who have suffered so much over the last 400 years inspires the hope that as we begin the fifth century of Virginia's history a new spirit of brotherhood is animating the commonwealth. If so, then Lynchburg's pioneer Quakers' faith in the potential of humankind finally will be vindicated.

Dorothy-Bundy T. Potter, Ph.D.
Clifton W. Potter Jr., Ph.D.

This volume is dedicated to Dr. Peter W. Houck who, in the last quarter of the twentieth century through his scholarly and philanthropic endeavors, realized anew some of the ideals that motivated the Quaker founders of Lynchburg. His 1984 work, *Indian Island in Amherst County*, helped rescue the Monacan Nation from obscurity and set it on the path to state and national recognition. A regular provider at the Free Clinic of Central Virginia, Inc., since its founding, his medical practice is now centered in the Johnson Health Center. Both entities make quality health care available to the less affluent residents of our region. He has also been the moving force in the creation of the Historic Sandusky Foundation, Inc., which purchased and will restore the house in which the fate of the city was decided during the Battle of Lynchburg in June 1864.

INTRODUCTION

The City of Lynchburg owes its genesis to the French and Indian War that began in 1756. The following spring, as colonists began to take advantage of the opening of the frontier, the Lynch family initiated its ferry service across the James at one of the few safe crossings in that treacherous river. Many of the pioneers who sought their services were bound for the virgin lands of the Ohio country that had been claimed by the French for over a century. With the end of hostilities in 1763, the victorious British closed their newly acquired western territories to colonization in an effort to placate local tribes. This directive would remain in force until the end of the American Revolution in 1783. During that 20-year period, settlers continued to move westward from the tobacco-depleted areas of eastern Virginia. They were looking for land to plant the "sovereign remedy" that had ensured the survival of Jamestown a century and a half earlier. They found the fertile rolling hills of the central Piedmont, and in 1786, the Quaker settlement was deemed large enough to be designated by the General Assembly as the town of Lynchburg.

Tobacco created the fortunes of Lynchburg. By 1840, the town was one of the most important stations on the James River and Kanawha Canal, and by 1855 the community was the second wealthiest city per capita in the United States, exceeded only by New Bedford, Massachusetts. During the secession crisis of 1861, Lynchburg opposed Virginia's leaving the Union, but with her inclusion in the newly created Confederate States of America, the city's sons and daughters served both in the field and at home. Because Lynchburg was a vital rail hub of the upper South, it became a major hospital center; hundreds of soldiers are buried in the Old City Cemetery, some from each state in the Confederacy.

With the coming of peace, the recovery of Lynchburg was rapid, as new industries replaced the financial dependence on tobacco. The diverse nature of the city's economy allowed it to weather the cycles of prosperity and depression that characterized the years from 1870 to 1940. During this same period, Lynchburg became a center for education with the founding of four colleges: Virginia Seminary and College, Randolph-Macon Woman's College, Virginia Christian College, and Sweet Briar College just outside the city in Amherst County. Virginia Seminary is now

Virginia University of Lynchburg, and VCC is now Lynchburg College. The city is also the home to four fine private scholastic institutions: Holy Cross School, Virginia Episcopal School, Lynchburg Christian Academy, and the Virginia School of the Arts. The public education system is one of the best in the state.

In the wars of the late nineteenth and twentieth centuries men and women from every racial, ethnic, and socio-economic group in Lynchburg made their contributions to the nation from the Spanish-American War to the Iraq War. Their sacrifice and service are commemorated in the memorials of Monument Terrace. That place of remembrance, which is the signature of Lynchburg, was featured on the reverse of the United States commemorative half-dollar struck in 1936 to mark its sesquicentennial recognition as a town. Only one other Virginia metropolis, Norfolk, has been so honored. On the obverse of this coin is the portrait of Lynchburg native Senator Carter Glass, a former secretary of the Treasury, and one of the authors of the Federal Reserve Act.

Many of the men and women who have called Lynchburg home for the last 250 years have made contributions to every realm of state and national endeavor. These range from the poetry of Anne Spencer, one of the gems of the Harlem Renaissance; the films of Randall Wallace, currently among the brightest young directors; to the performances of film star Carl Anderson and Faith Prince, one of Broadway's leading ladies. Social critics like Orra Grey Langhorne have paved the way for writers and scholars like Douglas Southall Freeman, Rebecca Yancy Williams, Robert D. Meade, Douglas Summers Brown, Peter W. Houck, James M. Elson, Darrell Laurant, G. Kenneth West, and S. Allen Chambers Jr. Bishop John Early established a pattern for community involvement for religious leaders that has included the Reverend Beverly Cosby and the Reverend Jerry Falwell. The list seems endless, and includes worthies in the arts, sciences, business, education, government, letters, the professions, and athletics.

As Lynchburg approaches the two hundred and fiftieth anniversary of its birth, it has added Central Virginia Community College and Liberty University to its roster of colleges. Our economy still demonstrates the ability to adapt, which has served the city so well as traditional industries have given way to technological innovation. As Lynchburg moves into the future, its citizens have reached back to maintain the best of the past. Since 1976, city leaders have created six historic districts preserving our architectural past. They include Point of Honor, an early nineteenth-century mansion house, and most recently all the structures on Rivermont Avenue, perhaps the oldest planned suburban community in the United States.

The early wealth of Lynchburg was founded in part on sweat and slave labor, but in the last quarter of the twentieth century her citizens embraced anew the principles of its Quaker founders—equality, diversity, and brotherhood. The City of Seven Hills has evolved into the City of Churches, and surely earned its place among Virginia's historic quadricentennial communities.

Of necessity, any history must be concerned with the cost of goods and services, and since Lynchburg was born on the banks of the James the value of the money used in daily commerce has inflated, deflated, and inflated again. To convert prices from the past into modern equivalents one should consult the most current edition of *The Value of a Dollar, Prices and Incomes in the United States, 1860–1999*, edited by Scott Derks. It takes $17.43 in 2000 dollars to equal the benchmark dollar of 1860; thus Jefferson's seemingly modest debt of $6,000 to a Lynchburg merchant becomes $104,580, and the $1,130 price for a slave becomes $19,696.

Chapter One

OMNINA

BEFORE 1757

Any serious study of central Virginia, and later the City of Lynchburg, must begin with a consideration of the impact of the Monacan Tribe upon this area. To begin a history of Lynchburg with its designation as a town by the Virginia General Assembly in 1786 is to ignore thousands of years of habitation by the peoples collectively known as First Nations, Native Americans, or Indians. When the first white adventurers penetrated the wilderness beyond the fall line of the river now known as the James, they encountered an ancient and highly organized culture, which Captain John Smith mentioned in his 1629 two-volume work, *The True Travels, Adventures, and Observations of Captain John Smith.* . . . His notes on and impressions of the Monacan were second-hand, based for the most part on the prejudice of their enemies, the Powhatan.

The Monacan are members of the Siouian language group, while the Powhatans speak a tongue that belongs to the rival Algonquin family. The name Sioux is actually a Chippewa word that means "foe" or "serpent." The nation that included numerous tribes and stretched from the Great Plains to the Atlantic Coast preferred to be called "Dakota," which means "friendly." While the Powhatan evolved a lifestyle that was centered on cultivating the fields, which surrounded an established village, the Monacan was in 1607 a more nomadic tribe of hunter/gatherers. From time to time, when game was scarce, they raided the fields of their Powhatan neighbors. Eventually they would cultivate the "three sisters"—corn, squash, and beans—in the clearings in the primal forests that were their home. Controlled burning of wooded land often created these open spaces. The charred areas quickly filled with savanna grass that attracted game, particularly deer and buffalo, and could be easily cleared for limited farming.

There was a balance of power among the various tribes until the arrival of the Europeans. The introduction of modern weaponry quickly destroyed this equilibrium, and in time led to the disappearance of some tribes and absorption of others by their stronger or more numerous neighbors. The story of how a remnant of the Monacans found a sheltered place of refuge, or *omnina* in the Dakota language, on the banks of the river where our community would be born, is the first chapter of Lynchburg's history.

It was not until the late nineteenth century that the Indians in central Virginia were identified with the Dakota. The history of the Algonquin after 1607 was familiar to laymen and scholars alike, and the tribes that formed the Iroquois language group, including the Cherokee, were well known. Generations reared on the story of Pocahontas and the novels of James Fenimore Cooper had very definitive notions of what Native Americans looked like and how and where they lived. The assumption that members of the Sioux nation ever called central Virginia home was dismissed as ridiculous. Well into the twentieth century many believed the Indians in the Lynchburg area to be Cherokee. Everybody knew the Sioux lived on the Great Plains and wore feathered war bonnets. Sioux warriors had annihilated General Custer and his troopers. In a series of articles published in the 1890s by the Bureau of American Ethnology, James Mooney speculated the tribes that separated the Algonquin from the Iroquois in Virginia were Dakota. The surviving remnant in the central part of the state was what remained of the once mighty Monacan Tribe. Recent archeological expeditions have confirmed Mooney's hypothesis concerning the Monacan.

In 1608, Christopher Newport, on orders from Captain John Smith, led a brief expedition into Monacan territory and visited two of the Monacan towns. Later, explorers were surprised to find these sites deserted or inhabited by other native groups. The nomadic nature of Monacan culture may account in part for the abandonment of these settlements, but there are other factors that must be considered as well.

In the first century after Jamestown, European diseases against which they had no natural immunity decimated the native population. Smallpox, tuberculosis, and even measles killed thousands, but particularly those in the prime of life. In some instances Europeans knowingly supplied Indians with items, particularly blankets, which had been contaminated by persons who had been infected with one of these deadly plagues. Whole tribes simply vanished, and the invaders claimed their ancestral lands. In the last analysis, microbes proved more deadly than firearms to the Indians of Virginia.

Native American and European concepts of land tenure and usage were diametrically opposed and resulted in the displacement of most of the Virginia tribes, for the Indian land was an asset held and used in common. One took from nature only what was needed for survival, and sharing was part of life. To Native Americans' regret, what they assumed was sharing the bounty of the land with the Europeans was in reality a loss of the resources upon which their survival depended. Again and again the white settlers, who took their land and pushed them ever westward towards the mountains, cheated the original inhabitants of Virginia. A nomadic tribe like the

Monacan was particularly vulnerable to this kind of systematic "legal" dispossession. Then there were the Iroquois.

Long before Europeans arrived, the Iroquois had a reputation for ferocity that inspired terror in their victims and enemies, especially the Monacan. When the Dutch armed the Iroquois with rifles, they unleashed a fury that led first to random raids against the Dakota, and then annual incursions into Virginia and the Carolinas. In their wake they left death, destruction, and slavery. The Monacan who survived these attacks fled deeper and deeper into the forests of central Virginia. Thus they came to the site of the future city of Lynchburg. Here the game was plentiful on hills that rose gently above the banks of the wide river and provided them with limited protection. The immediate ancestors of the Monacan of Amherst County were not the first Native Americans to fish these waters or camp on its edge, but they were the last. When they arrived, trappers and traders were pushing back the western limits of the English frontier.

The average colonist was unaware of the subtle differences that divided one Indian from another. To the casual observer all Native Americans were more or less alike. It is certainly true that the dwellings of the Monacan resembled the wickiup of the Powhatan. Flexible young saplings were bent in the shape of a large "U," and these pieces were lashed together using cross poles. The resulting framework resembled a large inverted basket. Strips of bark, woven mats, and deer pelts might be used to cover the frame producing a snug, although temporary dwelling. Shelves were lashed along the inner walls to provide sleeping and storage space. Smoke from the cooking and warming fires escaped from a hole in the roof. The wickiup could be dismantled, packed, and transported with relative ease, or due to the availability of building materials the framework could be abandoned while the skins and mats could be reused repeatedly.

The tribes designated as eastern Woodland adopted a style of dress that accommodated their environment. They decorated their bodies with natural dyes and practiced tattooing. While this form of personal decoration was considered beautiful, it also provided the wearer with a form of protective coloration permitting them to easily blend with their surroundings. Their clothing, particularly during the warmer months of the year, was minimal to allow easy passage through the forests, and since it was usually made from deer hide it also provided camouflage. An observant European might place Native Americans in their respective tribal groups by a familiarity with their hairstyles. While Monacan women favored long hair, the men cut their hair short. Decorative patterns used on clothing and in tattooing differed from tribe to tribe, or even sub-groups within a tribe. The Indians were quite familiar with these variations, which might mean the difference between life and death, but most white settlers were not. Language was the most obvious and easily recognizable distinction among various tribes. White settlers quickly gained a working knowledge of the language of the Indians who lived near them, but they also used the almost universal sign language favored by the Eastern Woodland tribes.

As contacts between the white settlers and their Native American neighbors increased, the differences among the various tribes became less distinguishable. This was due in part to the growth of trade. Blankets woven in Europe replaced those of deer or buffalo hide. Tools and weapons made of metal were preferred to those of stone and flint. Vessels of blown glass and pottery thrown on a wheel were substituted for woven baskets and traditional pottery. Slowly, Native Americans began to lose the ability to reproduce their traditional crafts as they became dependent, either by choice or circumstance, on the goods produced or provided by European settlers.

The Monacan were not involved in either the 1622 or the 1644 attempts by the Algonquins in Tidewater, Virginia, to massacre white settlers. Both efforts failed and led to reprisals against the Native Americans in that region. Bacon's Rebellion, however, indirectly affected them in 1676. Nathaniel Bacon is usually portrayed as a precursor of the War for Independence a century later. His "uprising" was in fact a personal power struggle with the governor. His followers directed their wrath against the First Nations to prevent the disappearance of the small independent farmer in the Chesapeake region of Virginia.

By 1619 there were Africans in Virginia, but their legal status is unclear. Some African immigrants entered as indentured servants on much the same footing as their white counterparts. When the terms of their indenture expired, blacks were free and received grants of land similar to those given to caucasians. There are still some black families in Eastern Virginia whose ancestors were never in permanent servitude. They trace their ancestry to these early indentured servants. With the Restoration of Charles II in 1660, and the return of Sir William Berkeley to his post as governor in Jamestown, the legal status of blacks in Virginia came into question. Soon perpetual slavery became the norm, and indenture was reserved for whites. The presence of a permanent black underclass helped transform the colony from that of a society dominated by small farmers to one controlled by a planter aristocracy. Bacon, who was one of those planter aristocrats, found it convenient to blame the Indians for the misfortunes of his neighbors, when in truth the real causes were slavery and depressed prices on the international tobacco market.

Bacon, who was an embarrassment to his family, immigrated to Virginia in 1674 to avoid a scandal at home. Sir William Berkeley's stubborn refusal to open territories reserved for the Indians to land-hungry small farmers left him politically vulnerable, and Bacon quickly used the plight of these dispossessed to advance his own political agenda, which eventually included the burning of Jamestown on September 10, 1676. As his movement began to lose momentum he took the radical step of promising freedom to all indentures and slaves who joined him. More than 100 took up his offer. Bacon's untimely death from dysentery led to the complete collapse of his "rebellion," and those farmers who refused to accept the victory of the great planters had only one real choice—migration westward. The indentures and slaves were soon recaptured and punished.

Thus by the end of the seventeenth century the lands beyond the fall line began to fill with settlers. First came the traders, then the surveyors, and finally farmers looking for a new start. For many of the Monacan this was the end, and they made the painful and irreversible decision to submit to the dominant tribe and become part of their confederation. This would mean the eventual loss of their dialect of Dakota and the subordination of their distinct culture to that of the Iroquois. However, a remnant of the Monacans refused to migrate northward and submit to absorption by their ancient enemy. They were the ancestors of the members of the Monacan tribe who still live at the Bear Mountain Settlement in Amherst County.

Any treaty arrangements that existed between the Monacan and the established white authority were made before the American War for Independence, and therefore any agreements reached with the British Crown were not legally binding on the new United States. Thus the government in Washington has never formally recognized the various Native American tribes in Virginia. It was not until 1989 that the Commonwealth of Virginia granted them formal status, but that in no way affected the position of the federal government. With no real definable status after 1781, the Monacan in central Virginia were forced to adapt to the dominant pattern of life, but until the 1820s they were able to live in relative obscurity and, for the most part, in harmony with their white neighbors.

The 1823 Virginia law known popularly as the "Mulatto Statute" cast doubt on the legal condition of persons of color, regardless of race, and especially those of mixed heritage. The fact that Thomas Jefferson in his *Notes on the State of Virginia* had suggested the blending of the white and red races counted for little now. The slave rebellion led by Nat Turner in 1831 in the eastern part of Virginia, and the hostile policy of the federal government towards Native Americans during the administration of Andrew Jackson, drastically altered the attitudes of many white Virginians towards their Indian neighbors. The once proud and independent Monacan were reduced not to slavery by these events, but to a seemingly permanent servile status that denied them their basic civil rights. They were forced to survive as tenants and servants to those persons who had once been their neighbors. Many chose to leave their ancestral home and attempted to blend into the general population.

Passing the color barrier was easy for some Monacan because they were the descendants of repeated marriages with whites. At contemporary gatherings of the Monacan, this varied heritage is still apparent. Some members of the tribe might easily change places with their forbears who roamed the forests of central Virginia, while others appear to be of European stock. The Monacan, like their fellow Native Americans, were a tolerant people who also offered sanctuary to blacks, either slave or free. Marriages with these new immigrants added another element into the heritage of the modern Monacan tribe. It also provided another excuse for the authorities to persecute central Virginia's Native American population.

The abolition of slavery after the Civil War had no effect whatsoever on the condition of the Monacan. They continued to survive on the margins of white society, but their status was about to change. In the last quarter of the nineteenth century, the ideas of the British naturalist Charles Darwin, particularly natural selection and the survival of the fittest, gave birth to doctrines that would almost destroy the Monacan. Herbert Spencer's Social Darwinism supplied the "scientific" justification for the domination of one group or nation over another. The German philosopher Frederick Nietzsche wrote at length about doctrines of race superiority, which in turn strongly influenced the development of the eugenics movement.

At the beginning of the twentieth century there were many in positions of power and influence who believed the authority of the state should be used to prevent "inferiors" from reproducing. The superiority of the white race was an almost universally accepted fact; all others were therefore subservient. In Nazism the most perverted form of eugenics was found, and it was not until after World War II that these ideas were fully discredited.

Dr. Walter A. Plecker, who became the first registrar of the State Bureau of Vital Statistics in 1912, attempted to commit bureaucratic genocide on the Indians of Virginia. In 1924, the Virginia Racial Integrity Law imposed Plecker's views upon the entire population of the state. All children born in the commonwealth were either white or black; there were no exceptions. Appeals by Native Americans were ignored, and according to the law they ceased to exist. Until his retirement in 1936, Plecker prosecuted his eugenics crusade against his perceived racial inferiors. It took another 36 years to dismantle the system that had such a devastating effect on the First Nations. Ironically, Plecker, the preeminent bureaucrat, regularly ignored traffic safety laws and thus he died at the age of 81 when he was hit by a car while crossing a Richmond highway.

The surnames most often associated with the Bear Mountain Settlement—Johns, Branham, and Redcross—began to appear on the Amherst County tax rolls almost from the time of its separation from Albemarle County in 1761. However, it was not until 1833 when William Johns purchased a large tract of land on Bear Mountain that the refuge for persons of Native American descent began to take form. Over the next half century most of the property passed out of the possession of his descendants on Bear Mountain, but many of them remained there; economic circumstances and the lack of educational opportunities essentially trapped them.

Until the 1870s, education, even the barest rudiments, was the privilege of those who could afford it. An examination of legal documents extant in the courthouses of Amherst County and Lynchburg attest to this fact. Many persons were unable to write their own names, and simply placed a mark that was certified by the proper clerk as a legal "signature." With the establishment of a system of public education in Virginia, the placement of Indian children in white schools was never seriously considered as an option. If they wished to obtain an education it could only be in schools created for black children. The Plecker system of birth registration made an appeal from this arrangement impossible. Thus it seemed that the Monacan had two choices: accept the dictates of the bureaucrats and deny their racial heritage, or embrace perpetual illiteracy. A schoolhouse existed at the settlement, but it was almost impossible to obtain a permanent teacher, and without continuity parents were not inclined to waste time on education. Children could and did provide a valuable labor force for their respective families, and thus by the age of 12 most youngsters were working eight to ten hour days. The future seemed bleak, but there was a third choice.

Most of the congregations established along the frontier before the Revolution were either Baptist, Methodist, or Presbyterian. The Episcopal Church, which was established by law as the only "legal" church, had no bishops resident in the colonies and thus missionary efforts were poorly organized or non-existent. With the coming of independence this changed, but in the minds of many Americans the Episcopal Church was still identified with the old order and the socially elite. However it is due to a resurgent Episcopal Church, a vital force for social change after the Civil War, that the rescue of the Monacan is credited.

At the very moment when W.A. Plecker's bureaucratic campaign began to be felt by the First Nations, Arthur Gray saw his work at the Bear Mountain Settlement take hold and begin to grow. Thanks to the Episcopal Church the Monacan had hope, albeit at times dim, during the dark days of segregation and official discrimination. As the son of one of the original Sweet Briar College faculty, Gray was encouraged by his father to devote his energies in the summer months to helping families that lived at Bear Mountain. Between 1908, when he graduated from the University of Virginia, and 1910, when he completed his studies at the Alexandria Theological Seminary and entered the Episcopal priesthood, Arthur Gray helped the Monacan build a church, expand their schoolhouse, and strengthen their sense of community.

St. Paul's, the name given the church at the Bear Mountain Settlement, was a mission congregation under the direction of the Bishop of Southwestern Virginia. While the rector of nearby Ascension supplied the Sacrament, a resident deaconess who was appointed by the bishop administered the authority of the church at the Settlement. Amherst County supplied a teacher for the mission school that provided an elementary education for the children of Bear Mountain.

One of the most important factors in the survival of Arthur Gray's shared dream was the involvement of "The Bum Chums," a group of students from Sweet Briar College. Generations of young women devoted their time, their energies, and their resources to supplement the assets provided by the church. When St. Paul's mission church and the home of the staff burned in 1930, the women of the college helped rebuild both structures.

Despite these positive changes, the Monacan at the Bear Mountain Settlement were still denied their identity by the state and their neighbors until the last quarter of the twentieth century. Commonly labeled as "Free Issues"—the descendants of slaves and the already racially mixed residents of the Bear Mountain Settlement—many younger members of the community decided to leave their ancestral home for places where they could finish their education and build a better life for themselves and their children. Then in 1952, Florence Cowan assumed the position of deaconess. When this devoted and indomitable advocate of the Monacan retired in 1965, many of the barriers erected to deny Amherst County's Indian residents their legal rights had fallen.

When the mission school closed in 1963, and the children of the Monacan entered the public school system, another chapter in the history of the tribe began. There was racial prejudice to overcome, and children can be unbearably cruel. No one who has not endured this kind of discrimination can really understand it. In a sense, the children who left the security of the Bear Mountain Settlement that fall were as brave as their ancestors who faced the fury of the Iroquois. Like the earlier Monacan, they brought honor to their tribe and blazed a trail that others still follow.

The Monacan tribe incorporated in 1988, the year before the Commonwealth of Virginia finally recognized the surviving tribes within its borders. Now with the

Mattaponi, Upper Mattaponi, Pamunkey, Chickahominy, Eastern Chickahominy, and the Nansemond, the Monacan are working to raise public awareness of the plight and potential of Virginia's Native Americans. There are 562 federally recognized tribes, but the Indians of Virginia currently are not among them. Working through VITAL (Virginia Tribal Alliance for Life), they are trying to change that.

The population at the Bear Mountain Settlement is now close to 900, and through the efforts of the tribal leaders, ancestral remains have been reburied at the settlement. The Monacan Ancestral Museum is maintained there, and a model village has been created at Natural Bridge for the education of the general public. Each year since 1993 the tribe has sponsored a pow wow, which is part reunion and part outreach. Almost four centuries after their ancestors found refuge in central Virginia, the modern Monacan hunt for bargains, not game, next to their neighbors of all races—thus fulfilling the ideals of the Quakers, the next group to find a home on these hills.

CHAPTER TWO

"QUAKE AND TREMBLE . . ."
1660-1786

While white explorers and trappers had penetrated central Virginia's primeval forests by the early 1670s, few attempted to build homes in the wilderness before 1700. By the mid-eighteenth century, however, small groups of Europeans— mostly English, Welsh, or Scottish—had begun farming along the James River (then called the Fluvanna) and nearby streams. A few Presbyterians had settled on Hat Creek in what was Lunenburg County in 1742. Shortly thereafter a village called New London was established by men more interested in land than in creating a godly community.

By 1746 New London was Lunenburg's county seat. Its modest collection of houses and shops, at least one tavern, and a magazine for securing weapons, powder, and shot elevated it to similar status when the new county of Bedford was created from Lunenburg in 1753. Thomas Jefferson, knowledgeable in many ways, predicted that two American communities, New London and New York, would in time achieve great things. As events proved, he was only half right.

No intimations of greatness seem to have been suggested for a small Quaker settlement that began beside the James River in the early 1760s. Even among the proliferation of nonconformist sects that had sprung from the political and religious confusion of the English Civil Wars, Quakers, or more correctly the Society of Friends, were conspicuous for the simplicity of their worship, their dedication to non-violence, proclamation of gender equality, condemnation of slavery, and their rejection of worldly titles and honors. Many in positions of authority deemed them deliberate subverters of social order, and pointed to their founder George Fox as an example of a dangerous man.

Born to a Leicestershire weaver in 1624 and apprenticed to a shoemaker, Fox was by nature contemplative and mystical and more anxious to fulfill a self-perceived void in his spiritual life than in earning a livelihood. In 1646, he experienced an inner voice that spoke of Jesus Christ as the Spirit or the Light, and in time he came to believe that the modes of worship deemed so essential to the Anglican Church or its Puritan counterparts were unnecessary hindrances to faith. One did not need a "hireling priest," hymns, or prayer books to come to an understanding of God.

"Quake and Tremble . . .": 1660–1786

In 1650, in one of his many spirited encounters with hostile authorities, Fox warned the judge to "quake and tremble before the Lord." "Ah ha," retorted Judge Gervase Bennet, "so you are one of those Quakers, are you?" Thus like the Methodists in the next century, Friends are best known by a name given them in derision.

In 1647, in the midst of the English Civil Wars, Fox began a travelling ministry, which continued until his death in 1691. In the process, he and his followers enraged Roundheads and Royalists alike. Friends spent years in prison, charged with heresy or disturbing the peace. They first refused to swear oaths of allegiance to the Cromwellian Commonwealth, and after 1660 to the Stuarts. While admiring Fox's tenacity, Oliver Cromwell as de facto military dictator of England from 1649 until his death in 1658 could not countenance a faith that espoused a refusal to bear arms.

The 1660 restoration of monarchy, Parliament, and the Anglican Church meant that persecutions of the Friends entered a different phase. Charles II, a tolerant king in an age of sectarian hatreds, pardoned 491 Friends in 1672; twice he issued Declarations of Indulgence (1662 and 1672), which decriminalized nonconformist worship outside the Church of England. Unfortunately, both declarations were voted down within months by the predominately Anglican Parliament.

During one of these brief periods of freedom from religious interference, Fox came to America, visiting Barbados, Jamaica, New England (where four Quakers had been hanged between 1659 and 1661), Maryland, Virginia, and North Carolina in 1671–1673. Those Friends and others whom he met lived in coastal towns and villages, not in the wilderness; yet still he saw some Native Americans and expressed concern for their souls and condemned the ill treatment they usually received from whites. Similarly, in Barbados, he saw first-hand the growing enslavement of Africans and admonished his white friends that Christ had died for all men and women, regardless of race. He also suggested that blacks should have terms of service like white indentures, and after these were completed they should be freed with sufficient resources to make a living.

Approximately 50 years after Fox's visit, a young Irishman indentured in Virginia would have reason to be grateful for the radically tolerant views of the Friends. It is unclear why Charles Lynch ran away from home at about age 15; various causes have been suggested, from an unfriendly stepmother to mistreatment in school. In any event, he persuaded a sea captain to take him to America, and about six weeks later the ship reached Virginia.

Like many poor adventurers before him, Charles Lynch was sold to pay his passage fees. The usual term of servitude was seven years; during that time the indenture was generally at the mercy of his or her master. Indentures worked alongside slaves and were likewise often abused; as long as they could be acquired cheaply their lives had little value. There were instances of indentures beaten to death by their owners for relatively minor infractions.

Charles Lynch was fortunate for he was bought by one of the Friends in Louisa County, Christopher Clark. Clark treated the young man kindly, and in time his daughter Sarah fell in love with him. They were married around 1733. Approximately 20 years later and shortly before his death in 1753, Charles, Sarah, and their family moved westward. "Chestnut Hill," their farm above the James River, was about a mile below the area that in less than four decades became the town of Lynchburg.

In wedding Charles, a Roman Catholic who apparently never became a Quaker, Sarah Clark "married out of Meeting" and as such was probably disowned by the Friends for a time. However, despite her marriage, Sarah Lynch was a member of the Camp Creek Meeting in Louisa County in 1750, and the six Lynch children were brought up in their mother's faith at Chestnut Hill. Three of them, John, Charles Jr., and young Sarah, would play significant and widely different roles in central Virginia's history. At least two Lynches remained true to their Quaker heritage, while one eventually chose to abandon it.

Enough Friends, including Sarah's two brothers, joined the family for worship so that the South River Monthly Meeting was established by 1757. The first meeting house was a log structure situated on land given by Sarah Clark Lynch. The building was in keeping with the spirit of those who constructed it. Quaker worship was the essence of simplicity, democracy, and equality. The Friends had no ordained clergy, no music or orders of service. Seating was separated by gender, but both men and women, such as Sarah Clark Lynch, could be elders. Members with unusual spirituality and gifts for speaking could be recommended as ministers, but they received no special entitlements or salary. Quakers came to their meeting house twice weekly: to worship together on Sundays, and to conduct business and disciplinary matters on Thursdays. Women and men met separately on Thursdays.

Even as the walls of the South River Meeting House were being raised 17-year-old John Lynch was engaged in a building project of his own. Pioneers moving westward into the Piedmont needed to cross the sometimes treacherous James River, aptly named for the mercurial James I. One of the better fording places was adjacent to land Edward Lynch, John's younger brother, had inherited on his father's death. In 1757, John began a ferry service across the river and in time expanded it to include a ferry house and tavern to facilitate the immediate needs of those he had transported.

The French and Indian War, which had just begun in 1756, was the catalyst leading to the genesis of Lynchburg. With the first permanent English settlement at Jamestown firmly established, and monarchy restored after the long and bitter Civil Wars, France replaced Spain as England's chief foe. They had been bitter enemies in the late Middle Ages, and at the end of the seventeenth century their rivalry, which would last until Napoleon's defeat at Waterloo in 1815, began again. Each Continental struggle had its North American counterpart. The War of the League of Augsburg (1688–1697) was King William's War in the colonies; the War of the Spanish Succession (1702–1713) they called Queen Anne's War; and the War of the Austrian Succession (1740–1748) was named King George's War. The first three conflicts had begun in Europe, but the French and Indian War commenced on the American frontier, and its European phase, the Seven Years War, was ultimately less important than the colonial struggle. Before ending in 1763, it involved military action on four continents, thus deserving to be designated as the first world war. Decisive battles were waged on American soil, and Great Britain's victory was complete.

Before 1756, Virginians who ventured to farm beyond the Blue Ridge Mountains risked their lives at the hands of the French and their Indian allies. The English were viewed as interlopers whose homesteads threatened the lucrative fur trade. They destroyed the habitat of the beaver, the lynx, and the otter. It is impossible to estimate the number of English settlers beyond the mountains who were killed or kidnapped and their houses destroyed. Britain's government could not protect them on lands claimed by the French. This situation changed with the beginning of hostilities in 1756. Suddenly the entire territory between the mountains and the Mississippi was in dispute, and more were willing to take the risk for a chance to lay claim to a homestead in the Ohio Country.

One of the most convenient routes westward lay through central Virginia. The Lynch brothers, led by John, furthered this migration with their ferry service. Over the next six years, thousands of settlers crossed the river and continued up the muddy trails above the water's edge. The Lynches' simple hostelry and storage facilities near their ferry landing grew into a thriving business run by men with a reputation for efficient and fair dealing.

Nineteenth-century Lynchburg citizens would compare their city to ancient Rome, because both were built on seven hills. A more accurate comparison is that both settlements were river-based and founded on commerce. It is unlikely that the Lynch family recalled the ancient Romans when they created their ferry service. An enterprising lot—there were no strictures against Quakers acquiring wealth through honest work—

they saw the revenue that could be gained by providing safe passage, food, and lodging for those on their way west. The river also nourished a tobacco culture, including the sale and shipment of the golden leaf down to the capital Williamsburg, and by the end of the century Richmond.

As the war accelerated, having a safe if temporary place to stay was no casual blessing on the edge of the frontier. Native Americans attempting to maintain their integrity and customs amid the struggle between the two European superpowers sided with France or Britain for their own advantages. The small number of remaining Monacans were uninvolved; not so the Shawnees, who raided British settlements along the Roanoke and New Rivers in 1755 and 1758. As in previous conflicts, Virginia Friends, like their co-religionists in Pennsylvania, refused to fight. Their neutrality was often incomprehensible to non-Quakers, most of whom collectively dismissed Indians as savages and pagans.

Some Friends did slip away to join local militias and when they returned home they were disciplined. John Echols, a long-time resident in Bedford County, was disowned by the Goose Creek Meeting in 1759 for joining a military company. Fear, self-preservation, and the lure of the forbidden created obstacles to Quaker pacifism; still the South River Friends had increased enough by 1763 to require an extension of their meeting house. When it burned in 1768 they built a larger wooden structure. Since many popular eighteenth-century amusements such as music, dancing, and card playing were forbidden pleasures, the meeting house was a social center as well as the focus of their religious activities.

At war's end in 1763, Great Britain was the most powerful nation in Europe, and her loyal subjects in North America looked forward to enjoying their share of her prosperity. Thirteen years later they would be embroiled in a struggle with the mother country that eventually included the formerly despised French as allies. Accounts of American Revolutionary battles have filled volumes. Understanding the "why" of the conflict is another matter.

The French and Indian War had left Britain with a tremendous national debt. William Pitt, Earl of Chatham, the main architect of Britain's worldwide strategy, had not allowed expenditures to trouble him—victory was his objective. Since the war had been fought in large part to protect British colonies in North America, the government felt it proper that Americans should pay their share. However, the colonists had for the most part managed their own affairs since 1619, and they resented being required to pay taxes levied without their consent.

George III had ascended the British throne in 1760 at the age of 22 with little preparation for leading an imperial state. One of his greatest weaknesses was an inability to choose able subordinates, and most of his ministers were as ill-prepared as he. Following the resignation of Chatham, whom he disliked, King George selected as his successors men who could be described at best as amateurs, and at worst as incompetents. They crafted the economic policies that drove the colonists into open rebellion and eventual separation from Great Britain.

With the passage of the Revenue Act of 1764, the British government tried vainly to correct abuses in the customs system while raising revenues for the defense of the colonies. Americans reacted by boycotting revenue-generating items mentioned in the act, such as imported wines, linens, and silks. In March 1765, parliament passed the Stamp Act, unleashing a furious protest that led to its repeal, as far as the colonies were concerned, exactly a year later. In June 1767, the Townshend Acts attempted to impose duties on tea, lead, glass, and paper bound for America. The revenues raised were supposed to pay the salaries of government officials in the colonies. Another boycott ensued, and in 1770 the government in London repealed all save the duty on tea. This led three years later to the Boston Tea Party.

These public acts of defiance were centered for the most part in the ports and towns near to the coast; those folk living near Lynch's Ferry were more concerned with the closing of the frontier. Beginning in 1762, pioneers were forbidden to settle on land beyond the sources of the rivers that flowed into the Atlantic Ocean.

Meant to placate tribes in the newly acquired French territories, as well as to encourage immigration by English-speaking settlers to Canada and Florida, the policy seemed sound and reasonable to those who formulated it in London. Colonists saw it as yet another attempt by absentee authorities to regulate their lives. The number of persons crossing at Lynch's Ferry dropped, but never stopped altogether. Some continued along well-worn tracks that led to the west and the southwest, while others saw central Virginia as a final destination. Among these were artisans whose skills were essential to the survival and growth of a settlement. Carpenter, blacksmith, joiner, cooper, tailor, cobbler, tinker—all were welcomed. Most were not Friends, and thus almost from the beginning of its history the majority of Lynchburg's population was nominally Protestant, but not Quakers.

Between 1756 and 1776 the population of Virginia almost doubled. While some of that quarter of a million inhabitants were native born, many were immigrants, especially Scots or Scotch-Irish. Used to hardships and distrustful of governmental authority, they tended to gravitate to the unregulated frontier. These new settlers probably brought the area's first slaves, but not in numbers found in the Chesapeake. A family might own one or two slaves who worked in the house, fields, workshop, or forge. During this same 20-year period, Virginia's African-American population increased by about 65 percent to around 200,000, or 40 percent of the total population. On the frontier it was easier to attempt to escape the bonds of slavery, and sometimes blacks found refuge among Native Americans who felt no obligation to return them to their white masters.

Slavery was one of three great concerns that began to strain the orderly existence the Friends tried to maintain among themselves and with their neighbors. The most immediate, armed rebellion against the British government, had clearly unacceptable implications; Friends did not take up arms, no matter how just a cause appeared to be.

Remaining neutral during the War for Independence was difficult. New London's magazine and Tory merchants were tempting targets for rebellious young men lured by dreams of military glory. Two of Virginia's heroes, Patrick Henry and Thomas Jefferson, had strong local ties. Still, most Friends refused to bear arms or hire a substitute to fight for them. Virginia law exempted Quakers from militia duty, but while their moral stance was legal, they were not spared the anger and contempt of their neighbors. This increased as Friends refused to engage in any activity related to the war, such as using Continental currency. Some even refrained from voting, since both sides were in conflict. Pacifists are generally a despised minority in wartime.

Charles Lynch Jr. was the most notable local Quaker to join the Patriot cause. He had first been disowned in 1769 for taking an oath as a burgess representing Bedford County. In 1775, he began to manufacture gunpowder and, along with friends, reopened a lead mine near Fort Chiswell in southwest Virginia to help supply weapons to Continental troops. In the summer of 1780, Colonel Charles Lynch and several other officers set up a military tribunal under a walnut tree at his farm "Avoca," now situated in the town of Altavista. Rumors of Tory raids on Charlottesville and New London, where 4,000 British prisoners were held, prompted Governor Thomas Jefferson to order the Virginia militia to take necessary precautions. A number of captured Tories were imprisoned in Bedford; others were marched to Avoca and summarily judged, tied to the tree, and whipped. Their punishment was reduced if they would cry "Liberty forever."

This harsh treatment became known as "Lynch's Law." In 1782, when several of his victims sued for damages, the Virginia General Assembly officially excused the actions of Lynch, his fellow Colonels James Calloway and William Preston, and Captain Robert Adams Jr. There is no record of hangings at Avoca; however the term "lynch law" became a synonym for mob injustice, usually hangings, particularly inflicted upon African Americans. There is no record of a lynching ever occurring in Lynchburg.

The Revolution's end in 1783 removed one stress from Quaker life, at least until the War of 1812, when a number of men, including Charles Lynch, were disowned.

However the issue of slavery was not to be resolved in a few years' time. George Fox's condemnation was echoed by Friends throughout America. Members of the South River Meeting, calling for the end of slavery in Virginia, were led by Sarah Lynch Terrell until her death in 1770. Two years later, in 1772, the Yearly Meeting declared that any Friend who bought or sold a slave should be disowned; in 1775 they forbade ownership altogether, as well as hiring another's slave, a common practice for slaves with skills like carpentry or bricklaying. Records from the Cedar Creek and South River Meetings between 1780 and 1835 list members who were disowned for "holding a slave," or "overseeing slaves."

This was more than supporting a noble cause in an abstract sense. By freeing their slaves, and encouraging others to do so, Virginia Quakers had for all practical purposes destroyed their means of livelihood and their social status. Most were farmers whose major crops were labor-intensive tobacco and corn. The old indenture system no longer existed. Even if a Quaker family had many sons, it was socially unacceptable for white nineteenth-century Southerners to work their fields. Moreover, such a family could not compete with the unfree labor of their neighbors.

Few other economic options existed; Friends had no paid clergy, they could not teach music, run a distillery, become tailors, dressmakers, or create beautiful but worldly decorative goods. Indeed, Quakers were frequently disowned for using "spirituous liquors" or "following vain fashions." Their non-Quaker neighbors saw emancipation as illegal according to the laws of the state and as a threat to their way of life, which they justified by select passages from the Scriptures.

A considerable number of Quakers found the economic sacrifices and social isolation that were part of emancipation efforts simply too difficult, so they kept their slaves, were disowned, and joined other denominations. Many became Methodists or Baptists and remained in Lynchburg after their more resolute brothers and sisters moved westward to territories that would become Indiana, Ohio, Kansas, and even Oregon and California.

A third problem Quakers found increasingly difficult to combat as it began impinging on their numbers was "marrying out of unity." Even Sarah Clark Lynch, who had contributed materially and spiritually to the fledgling settlement that became Lynchburg, repeated the transgression in 1766. Her second husband, Major John Ward, was like the late Charles Lynch—a Catholic. Worse still, he was a military man.

While records of the Cedar Creek and South River Meetings indicate that both men and women Friends married out of their faith, disownments as listed in J.P. Bell's *Our Quaker Friends of Ye Olden Time* show nearly twice as many women as men choosing non-Quaker marriage partners. The modesty and gentleness of Quaker girls were attractions, and for some female Friends a desire for a less restrictive life may have been as alluring as thoughts of love. Regardless of reasons, the results were serious; a dwindling reproductive population dooms any social group to potential extinction. The Friends refused to compromise, and as the area became more populous, temptations and disownments mounted. These included:

> Peter Holland, "disowned for worshipping with Baptists" (1767)
> Micajah Clarke. . . "frequenting places of sport and gaming" (1770)
> Barzilla Barnard. . . "fighting, swearing, and drinking." (1788)
> Samuel Harrison, "joining the Masons and marching to music" (1794)
> Betty Johnson. . . "dancing and attending places of diversion" (1799)
> Thomas Johnson, "drinking, fighting, and hiring a slave" (1802)
> Asa Wood, "playing cards, taking oaths, joining the Masons" (1821)

An erring Friend who wished to be reinstated had to write a confessionary letter to his or her meeting, asking for forgiveness for the specific fault and promising to not repeat the offense. Many of these still survive in Quaker records. It is worth noting that even John Lynch was at least once disowned by the meeting established on his family's land. In a humble letter submitted for the South River Meeting's consideration in September 1787, he admitted that he had "given way to a spirit of resentment." This attention paid to what most would consider a trivial offense shows the depth of character of Lynchburg's Society of Friends.

Chapter Three

"THE SEAT OF SATAN'S KINGDOM"

1786–1852

By 1786, there were enough Quakers and other settlers near the ferry to form a town. Since John Lynch agreed to make 45 acres available, naming it was easy. In October, the Virginia General Assembly gave John and Charles Lynch and nine other trustees the right to survey and sell lots of half an acre, "with convenient streets, and to establish a town by the name of Lynchburg." The land was not a gift; John Lynch was reimbursed as lots were sold.

The ferry house, a tobacco warehouse, and a mill on Blackwater Creek, all owned by John Lynch, were among the town's first structures. Four streets, Lynch, Water, Second, and Third, plus four numbered alleys, were laid out in a grid. This central core in time became the heart of Lynchburg's business district, but at first growth was slow and sporadic, due in part to problems experienced by the entire nation, which was in crisis in the 1780s.

Devastated by war, deprived of the economic benefits of being part of Britain's empire, plus its naval protection, the United States was in debt to everyone from the French to its own soldiers and officers. A Depression in 1784–1785 was worsened by inflated paper currency issued by various states at differing standards of value. Congress was unable to raise sufficient revenue, much less command international respect. Central authority under the Articles of Confederation was diffused and ineffective, fostering rivalries among larger states like Virginia, Pennsylvania, and New York.

A Constitutional Convention met in Philadelphia to deal with these and other problems in the spring and summer of 1787, and ratification of the new Constitution by New Hampshire the following June set in motion the genesis of a stronger central government. These events, coupled with the inauguration of George Washington as first president in April 1789, inspired national confidence and proved to be forerunners of growth for new towns like Lynchburg. In the early 1790s, the town had at least 20 large houses as well as smaller dwellings, and more than a dozen stores. These often doubled as residences, with the owner and his family living above the ground floor commercial space. By 1800, Lynchburg had about 500 inhabitants, so two years later John Lynch provided 30 more lots at its southeast and northwest limits. Three additional alleys connected these new lots with the old.

Dwellings during this period included one-room log cabins with dirt floors for the poor or slaves or, more typically, cottages of white-washed riven siding with rough board floors and interior walls filled with "nogging," a form of insulation made of mud, straw, and debris from construction. Roofs were often cedar tiles or shakes, readily available in central Virginia. Furniture in the main room usually included a bed, with a loft under the roof providing additional sleeping space.

Chimneys in simpler dwellings were made of caulked logs that often caught fire; in more finished houses they were stone or brick. Those who could not afford window glass used oiled paper; shutters kept out rain, cold, and flies. As Lynchburg grew, these modest buildings gave way to brick houses of several stories with painted trim and siding and outbuildings: stables, barns, a kitchen, woodshed, and meat house. An older structure might be contained within the walls of its replacement, with additions supplying the needs of the next generation of residents.

While the major streets were paved in Philadelphia, America's most famous Quaker community, Lynchburg's residents had to contend with narrow dirt tracks that depending on the season were potential storms of red dust or seas of mud. To improve the busiest streets, trees were cut, split, and laid side by side, producing a corduroy effect. Boardwalks kept pedestrians out of the worst mud or dirt.

There was no sewer system. Pigs freely roamed the streets consuming all sorts of waste; they in turn were eaten. Pork was the cheapest and most readily available meat because the animals were so self-sufficient. By 1811, Lynchburg employed a pig catcher. His duties also included rounding up stray dogs which, unlike pigs, added little to town life.

Faith had been essential to Lynchburg's beginnings; yet there was no church within its limits for 20 years. From 1792 to 1798, the South River Friends constructed their third and final meeting house. Built of fieldstone, it remained outside the city until the twentieth century. The same was true for a small Anglican Chapel; dating from about 1765, it was abandoned after the Revolution, briefly became a private school, and burned in 1802.

Travelling Methodist evangelists preached in private homes, the open air, or at the Masons' Hall. Built around 1794 for Marshall Lodge Number 39, and organized the previous year despite Quaker disapproval of Masonic secret rites and public parades, Masons' Hall was the town's primary gathering place for decades. But it was not a church. Troubled by this lack of spirituality, the famous preacher Lorenzo Dow described Lynchburg in 1804 as "the seat of Satan's Kingdom."

This dubious distinction existed for years, as the number of taverns and ordinaries increased. In 1806, a year after Lynchburg's incorporation, local Methodists raised enough money to build the first church inside the town limits, on what in time became Church Street. In 1807 they organized a large camp meeting, and the next year they held a conference in Lynchburg.

Some found camp meetings, an essential part of the "Second Great Awakening," disturbing. Begun in the late 1790s, this religious phenomenon lasted into the 1820s. Large groups of men, women, and children, both white and black, flocked to revivals that lasted for days. Participants moaned, shouted, wept, jerked, and fainted. Such raw emotionalism and a collapse of customary social norms, for a few preachers were African Americans, offended traditionalists. James Graham, editor-publisher of the weekly *Lynchburg Star* from 1805 to 1811, described the Reverend Stith Mead, a leader of the Methodists who also edited the rival *Lynchburg Press*, as a "hypocrite," and "a contemptible, vaporing, itinerant brawler."

Voting, like religion, was treated with great seriousness by the first generations of post–Revolutionary Americans, though only white males were part of the process. The town crier walked the streets ringing his bell to remind those eligible to go to Masons' Hall to vote. This polling site changed in January 1813 with the completion of the town's first courthouse, a brick structure built on a lot John Lynch had deeded to the city in 1805.

For a few weeks the courthouse had a major problem overlooked by the building committee and the town council: it was outside the town limits. This might have led to some interesting legal challenges, but in February 1813 the general assembly allowed the town to annex its own courthouse, the 16-foot square log jail behind it, a pillory, and a whipping post. A log jail seems odd, but its plank floors and walls were spiked with iron bars to frustrate escapes. Without fireplaces and with minimal light, it was meant for brief incarcerations, rather than rehabilitation.

By 1814 Lynchburg's two banks were definite proofs of its rising affluence, thanks to increased cultivation and sales of tobacco. Five tobacco warehouses were built between 1801 and 1805 alone, at about the same time as the town's first factory, which produced chewing tobacco, was constructed. For more than a century the long, low, and sturdy warehouses served many purposes; they were sites for agricultural fairs beginning in 1837, and venues for political rallies and banquets. During the Civil War they became hospitals. When the tobacco market shifted southward to Danville, their foundations were used for other buildings such as Lynchburg's premier theater, the Academy of Music, which opened in 1905.

Visitors to Lynchburg often commented on its tobacco-based wealth. One of the most noted—or notorious—was Anne Royall, who shared James Graham's dislike of enthusiastic preachers. This caustic lady-journalist visited Lynchburg in January

1830, and while awed by its scenery, which she called "the most rich and varied . . . of which any town in the Union can boast," she lamented in her southern tour that "this heavenly spot is cursed with the terror of our land, Priest-craft and Missionaries!!"

The town now had six churches: two Methodist, two Baptist, one Presbyterian, and one Episcopal; all built by whites. Blacks, free or slave, held informal worship under trees, in brush and bush arbors, or sat in the balcony of white churches. They were the backbone of the 15 tobacco factories, which employed around 450 slaves, and seven warehouses. Mrs. Royall also observed the numerous low flat-bottomed batteaux carrying goods between Lynchburg and Richmond. Many of those manning these boats, requiring strength and river-knowledge, were African-Americans.

The James remained vital to the town's existence, but urban growth and the river's unpredictability created problems. A fire company had been organized in 1799 to combat the frequent blazes in houses lit by candles and lamps, and also to sink wells and install public pumps. Occasionally the river almost ran dry and local springs and wells were not adequate. Around 1810, the town council authorized John Lynch Jr. to supply water from springs on his property, through log pipes reinforced with iron bands. By 1818 this was insufficient, and a nine-foot wooden reservoir was constructed on Church Street. It cost $600, and leaked continually.

New entertainments supplemented old favorites like gaming, horse racing, cock fighting, and dancing. In 1805, a travelling show with a female elephant came to Lynchburg. Children paid 12.5¢ and adults 25¢ to see the exotic beast. These sums were not trivial; a child's ticket cost as much as a quart of milk or a single music sheet, and 25¢ was about half a day's wage for a working man.

Balloon ascensions (dating from the 1783 invention by the Montgolfier brothers in France) were exciting and, unlike a circus or the tightrope walker who performed at the Mason's Hall in March 1802, viewing was free. Although early balloons were unmanned, the ascent of one of these colorful silk bags would bring out the town. Sent aloft from a hill called Black's Lot, they floated toward the James, gradually losing altitude as the hot air cooled. On one occasion a balloon passed over the river and dropped by the home of an elderly lady who thought the end of the world had come, and that she was about to be transported to Heaven in a chariot of fire.

Festive occasions were also linked to national events. An 1806 Independence Day celebration recounted in the *Lynchburg Star* began with a cannon being fired, a militia drill, and martial music (presumably most Quakers stayed home). In the evening there was an "elegant barbecue" and a ball held at the Bell Tavern. When civic or military heroes passed through town, including General Andrew Jackson in April 1815 and Henry Clay in September 1828, similar honors awaited them. Jackson, the hero of the battle of New Orleans, was entertained with a reception and public banquet at the courthouse, hosted by former president Thomas Jefferson. After the festivities, both men rested at the Bell Tavern before going to Poplar Forest, Jefferson's Bedford County retreat.

Lynchburg citizens considered Jefferson one of their own. In retirement he spent more time at nearby Poplar Forest, and had many friends and business associates in the area. On one trip through Lynchburg he is reputed to have stopped at the garden of Mrs. Owen Owen, whose pride was a fine crop of Italian-style tomatoes, or "love apples" as they then were known. When he asked Mrs. Owen for one, she thought it was for his extensive collection of plants. Instead Jefferson ate it. Believing that tomatoes were poisonous ornamentals, Mrs. Owen was frantic; the author of the Declaration of Independence and former president was about to die in her garden! Jefferson laughed and assured her that tomatoes were perfectly safe to eat. Popular tradition claims this was the first time a tomato was eaten in central Virginia. In commemoration, a "Tomatoe Faire" has been held each summer at the City Market since 1976. Entries are judged on size, flavor, and unusual shapes.

Unless wealthy and well-traveled like Jefferson, one's choices of food and drink in early nineteenth-century Virginia were limited. Streams and wells were often polluted by farm animals or outdoor privies, so most people preferred cider, beer, or ale. Older children drank beer or cider mixed with water, while young children and people with stomach complaints were given milk. Babies might be breast-fed until one or two years of age, as a primitive form of birth control. Women or men might be brew masters, but later in the century brewing became a predominately male occupation.

Indian corn or "maize" was America's major food source. Corn cakes, corn mush, or "Indian" puddings were eaten daily. Fish were dipped in corn meal and fried; corn was fed to farm animals, and made into whiskey. Producing "corn liquor" or "moonshine" was common, since it was easier and more profitable to turn surplus corn or rye into alcohol than to transport it over rough roads to market. Rural Americans had deeply resented the federal excise tax on whiskey in 1791. Western Pennsylvania's "Whiskey Rebellion" in 1794 was quickly defused when President Washington confronted the protesters with a large militia, asserting the government's right to levy taxes. Taxed or untaxed alcohol was a staple in Lynchburg's taverns, those "places of diversion," so objectionable to the Friends. One Main Street establishment called The Eagle was renamed The Buzzard by locals. Perhaps it was the food.

Weather phenomena always offer conversational gambits, and 1816 gave people throughout America strange stories they would tell for decades. The so-called "Year without a summer" began normally, but April and May's storms and frost killed crops and even flocks of migrating birds. Snow fell in June after a lunar eclipse, frost covered the ground in July and August, and September and October felt like December. A large sunspot also appeared, leading pious souls to speculate on signs that the end of the world was near.

Americans were unaware that the bizarre weather was the result of a natural disaster the previous year. On April 7, 1815, Mount Tambora on the Indonesian island of Sumbawa exploded, killing more than 10,000 people with falling volcanic debris, earthquakes, or tsunamis. As ash and sulfur particles in the atmosphere gradually overspread the earth, global temperatures dropped, resulting in crop failures and famine. Virginia was less affected than New England, but much of its wheat, hay, and corn crops were destroyed. September brought heavy rains, particularly to Petersburg and Appomattox. Seemingly there were only two benefits to the local economy: the tobacco crop survived, and the cold killed the flies.

1817 brought no more climatic surprises, but rather the first stirrings of a transportation revolution. In April, the Lynchburg and Salem Turnpike Company was organized and soon stage coaches appeared on a regular schedule. This in turn encouraged the building of better lodging for visitors. In November, the Franklin Hotel opened its doors on Main (formerly Second) Street, near where Lorenzo Dow had preached on sin. In size, furnishings, and food it was said to equal any other hotel in Virginia. Jefferson, a close friend of the owner Samuel Harrison, advised him on which imported wines should be purchased for its cellar.

In addition to excitement about the hotel, rumors flew that Lynchburg might become the site of the new University of Virginia. After all, Mr. Jefferson had important connections to the town. In 1818, Main Street was paved with "river jack" cobbles of sandstone, and there was a brief but feverish land boom. Hopes were dashed when, not surprisingly, Charlottesville was chosen instead. Jefferson's whole life had been centered in Charlottesville and Albemarle County, therefore it was only natural that he would want his "Academical Village" to be built close to the spot he called home. Lynchburg and Poplar Forest were his places of rest and retreat.

With the inconsistency common to human nature, Jefferson, the advocate of yeoman farmers as linchpins of American democracy, was himself an improvident aesthete. Monticello and Poplar Forest's visitors marveled at his imaginative architecture, his inventions and agricultural experiments, his library, and his elegant cuisine. But all these things came with a two-fold price. Jefferson's lifestyle, far beyond that of the average Virginian, was based on a large slave labor force. Also, unable to resist acquiring more books, the best harpsichord, or finest piano for his daughters and granddaughters, Jefferson constantly found himself in debt.

William Brown and Archibald Robertson, who ran Lynchburg's first dry goods store, learned about Jefferson's absence of economy firsthand. They sold tea, coffee, sugar, molasses, blankets, cloth, and other goods, extended credit, and served as informal bankers for their best customers. The patronage of so notable a man as Jefferson must have initially delighted them, but they were to be disappointed. Apologies, promises of payments, and hopes for better times were frequent themes in Jefferson's letters to Robertson (Brown had died in a Richmond theater fire in 1811).

Admittedly the War of 1812 created economic hardships for many Americans; however, Jefferson's debts mounted at an extraordinary rate. After his death, Archibald Robertson, to whom Jefferson still owed $6,000, became one of the appraisers for Poplar Forest, and doubtless soon discovered the extent of the former president's debts was much greater than he had imagined.

Many Lynchburgers knew of Jefferson's financial difficulties, and in the spring of 1826 a number of citizens met at the Franklin Hotel to form a committee to collect funds on his behalf. These gifts were to be presented on July 4, the fiftieth anniversary of the Declaration of Independence—and ironically, the day Thomas Jefferson died at Monticello. On July 20, the town held a dual memorial service for Jefferson and ex-president John Adams who had died the same day, and as a mark of respect citizens agreed to wear a mourning arm band of black crepe for 30 days.

Jefferson and Adams were icons, visible links to national greatness, but the gradual demise of the Friends' historic legacy was by and large lost on Lynchburg. The last recorded marriage at the South River Meeting House took place in 1828. By 1843 its Worship and Monthly Meetings were discontinued. The westward migration of the Friends and the rise of racial and sectional rhetoric meant even fewer options for Virginia's African Americans.

A 1782 state law allowing owners to emancipate their slaves had initially raised the number of Virginia's free blacks. Even non-Quakers often supported emancipation for specific slaves, the elderly, the better educated, or those with particular skills. For example, "Blind Billy" Armistead, a popular Lynchburg black musician, would be freed shortly before his death in 1855.

Free-born African Americans, and those who had been freed, often had relatives who were still enslaved. Since it was customary to pay slaves for overtime work, buying freedom for one's family was possible, but it took a long time and depended to some extent on a master's willingness to release valuable property. However, between 1810 and 1820 free blacks made up between 10 and 11 percent of Lynchburg's total population, and between 22 (in the 1810 census) and 26 percent (the 1820 census) of all African Americans in town. This decade saw the largest percent of Lynchburg's free blacks before the Civil War; by 1850 they made up only seven percent of the population.

Freedom was not equality with whites. Free blacks had to register at a local court; they could not vote, own guns, or become ministers or teachers. Voting and firearm bans were strictly enforced, but even though black churches had to have a white minister, there were African-American preachers from colonial times onward. Blacks were also not supposed to be literate, but some masters ignored this law. Hannah, Jefferson's slave housekeeper at Poplar Forest, wrote him a brief letter in 1818, expressing concern for his health. John Hemmings, his master carpenter, also wrote from Poplar Forest in 1825 about specific alterations to the house.

Post-1806 emancipation in Virginia was greatly affected by the first law of its type in the United States requiring every slave freed after May of that year to leave the state within 12 months of emancipation or be reenslaved. There was a provision that individuals could petition the general assembly for permission to remain, but the complex process needed white cooperation. In 1816 the general assembly granted local courts authority to determine or deny permanent residence for free blacks initially within their jurisdiction; in 1837 this applied in the state.

Men, women, and children of color were sold in Lynchburg at the Indian Queen Tavern and in front of the City Market; both were on Main Street. Whites troubled by this cruelty sought solutions. In 1823, the council passed an ordinance prohibiting the buying and selling of slaves within town limits, but found that under state law they could only regulate sales, not prohibit them.

Another option was returning blacks to Africa. The American Colonization Society (ACS), established in 1817, acquired territory in West Africa and named it Liberia. Lynchburg's branch of the ACS, organized in 1825, had over 100 members, including Methodist Bishop John Early and Mayor John Victor.

Most southern whites and a few blacks found colonization logical. Unlike Indians, America was not the Africans' native land, and their color and long history of servitude singled them out in comparison to other immigrants like the Irish or the Jews. Nat Turner's bloody rebellion in 1831 in Southhampton County further convinced many whites that returning blacks to Africa was the best solution for everyone. However, most free blacks, particularly in towns and cities, had no interest in rural Liberia; it was not their home, they and their ancestors had helped build America, and they resisted separation from family and friends. The colonization movement peaked in the 1830s and in time failed because not enough whites or blacks truly supported it.

In the 1820s and 1830s, the river offered a major challenge and a significant opportunity for Lynchburg. The challenge was creating an adequate water supply;

developing faster transportation was the opportunity. First on the agenda was the water problem. The now-demolished wooden reservoir was proof that outside expertise was needed. In 1825, a committee chaired by Mayor John Victor hired Albert Stein, a noted Philadelphia civil engineer, to recommend solutions.

In seeking advice from Philadelphia, Lynchburgers were not just building on an obvious Quaker connection, for Philadelphia's gravity water system was famous. Recently completed in 1823, it brought water by aqueducts from the Delaware and Schuylkill rivers through a system of pipes and hydrants. Stein visited Lynchburg and drew up a plan, which Victor presented to council in February 1827. It included construction of a 600,000-gallon reservoir on the site of the old fair ground, a dam on the south side of the river, and a canal to carry water to a pumping station at the bottom of Seventh Street hill. The pumping station would force water up to the reservoir through iron and wooden pipes. Skeptics were dubious. Costs were estimated at $50,000, and the city had budgeted only $10,000. Besides, water could not flow uphill.

An adventurous, or desperate, council approved the plan on June 29. Funds were borrowed, the necessary properties secured, and work began. Despite the optimism of the water committee, especially Victor and Bishop John Early, public opinion began turning against the project. By the time construction was finished and the trial day set for July 18, 1829, threats of tar and feathers or even hanging were being sent to Early and Victor.

At the appointed hour, a large crowd was in place by the reservoir; the pump was started, but no water gushed forth. As people began to murmur, a small boy named George Thurman agreed to be lowered down the main pipe to listen for the water. The first time he was pulled up, he said there was only a roaring sound; the next time he was covered with blowing dust. As he was lowered a third time, he had barely gotten out of sight before he screamed, "Draw me up quick!" Out came George, and up came the water. Victor, Early, and the rest of the water committee were vindicated. Lynchburg's waterworks remains the second oldest gravity system in the nation.

The second river project was a canal. Britain had moved goods and people on canals since the mid-eighteenth century, and the Erie Canal begun in 1817 eventually stretched 28 miles. In 1832, the general assembly authorized a canal that was supposed to go from Norfolk through Lynchburg to the Kanawha River and on to the Ohio. However, construction was painfully slow; the first canal barge did not reach Lynchburg until 1840. Once opened, trips from Lynchburg to Richmond via canal took only two days, but they cost $8. Ultimately, the canal ended in 1851 in Buchanan, not at the Ohio, and was replaced by faster and more efficient railways.

LYNCHBURG

Even before incorporation of the canal, Lynchburg wanted a railroad. In 1831, and again in 1835, plans were promoted for a rail line to southwest Virginia, but both were defeated by the state legislature committed to the canal project. Finally, in November 1847 at a public meeting, the town voted to build its own line and to subscribe $500,000 in stock themselves. After arguing for more than six months with the General Assembly on the legality of such a move, Lynchburg's line was approved and even provided some funding, but the price was a name change. The Lynchburg and Tennessee Railroad became the Virginia and Tennessee. Ground was also broken for a line to Petersburg in January 1850, the same year Lynchburg's population passed 8,000 people.

By mid-century the town was being transformed in ways early residents could only have imagined. Houses and businesses became brighter and more safely illumined, thanks to the creation of the Lynchburg Gas Light Company in March 1851. By December 1852 it had 29 customers, and some gas lamps were in place on major streets within two more years. The Lynchburg and Abingdon Telegraph Company was organized in August 1851, and four months later Lynchburgers had their first daily newspaper, *The Daily Express*. On February 18, 1852, Lynchburg's first railway engine, "the Virginia" chugged into town. It was time to assume new status; Lynchburg officially became a city on August 27, 1852.

Chapter Four

"THE METROPOLIS OF

SOUTHWEST VIRGINIA"

1852–1861

On May 20, 1852, the Virginia General Assembly passed the bill declaring Lynchburg a city, and on August 27 of that year, after several changes were made in the document, the revised charter took effect. This momentous event should have been a cause for celebration; instead it coincided with an incident that was both a tragedy and a comedy.

The ramshackle Market House, which had been built on Ninth Street between Main and Church Streets in 1814, had become something of an eyesore, and stray dogs daily collected to feed on the offal and garbage discarded by the merchants who did business there. These animals posed a threat to the public well-being because they might carry a number of diseases, including the almost always fatal "hydrophobia," or rabies, for which there was neither a preventive treatment nor a cure. In an effort to control the growing canine population, the council passed an ordinance that taxed all dogs owned as pets, and empowered the police to destroy all those not duly licensed and not on lead. Immediately, the constabulary seemed to have exceeded its commission in an effort to remove once and for all a public nuisance. There were dead dogs everywhere, strays and pets alike. The citizens reacted without delay. Dressed as Indians and under cover of darkness they dumped the carcasses on the lawns of the members of council, reserving the largest number for Charles W. Christian, the author of the ordinance. Smarting from this public rebuke, the entire council resigned. However, a citizens' meeting asked them to reconsider, which they did. They reassumed their duties, the charges against the policemen were dropped, and life in the new city returned to normal. However, the fate of the dead dogs is not recorded.

By 1855 Lynchburg was the second wealthiest city per capita in the United States, surpassed only by New Bedford, Massachusetts. Its wealth was built on the whaling industry, while Lynchburg's was founded on the manufacturing of "plug" or chewing tobacco. There were 30 tobacco factories in Lynchburg in 1850; by 1860 there would be 15 more, employing 1,054 or 15.4 percent of the total population of 6,853. Other than white overseers, the majority of these workers were black slaves. Thus Lynchburg's wealth was built on labor that was not free.

LYNCHBURG

The proportion of free blacks in the population of Lynchburg had declined since 1820, but they were skilled craftsmen who, like the poorest whites, would not demean themselves by working in the tobacco factories. Slaves were rented by their masters to the factory owners on an annual basis, but they could earn from $3 to $5 per week for "overwork," and it was theirs to keep. By 1860, 40 percent of the city's population was black, and those slaves not forced to work in the factories were usually in domestic service. It is impossible to accurately calculate how many middle and upper class households were served by these men and women, but some estimates were close to 50 percent. Thus by the time of the secession crisis, forced servitude was firmly established in Lynchburg.

Slaves to be sold were kept in "Woodruff's Jail" on Lynch Street, now Commerce Street, between Ninth and Tenth Streets. Shortly before the war, Seth Woodruff realized prices for the human beings in his charge, ranging from $640 to $1,130. It is ironic that while Woodruff was selling many of these men, women, and children to plantation owners in the cotton states of the deep South, apologists for slavery maintained that those in bondage were grateful to be spared the privation of the poor whites. However, these writers never stopped to consider that freedom for those who do not possess it is more precious than any material goods.

On April 2, 1855, John Notman of Philadelphia was hired by the council to plan a new burying ground outside the city to be known as Spring Hill Cemetery. It was considered healthier to bury the dead far from any public water source, and Lynchburg's new status demanded that its contemporary city of the dead be designed by the best landscape architect and in the latest style. The neighbors of the proposed facility were outraged and threatened to prevent its use. Six months later, on October 18, Howell Robinson was the first person to be buried in Spring Hill Cemetery, with an armed escort that proved unnecessary.

On May 25, 1855, the new courthouse was finally finished at a cost of $22,000. Designed by W.S. Ellison, a division engineer with the Virginia and Tennessee Railroad, it was built by the local firm of Hallet & Mace. When Lynchburg's status changed from that of a town to a city in 1852, it was painfully obvious to all that the municipality needed a modern courthouse to replace the old dilapidated one. Ellison's design was accepted by the Committee of the Common Council on March 19, 1853. The courthouse was supposed to be finished by June 1, 1854, at a cost of $18,000. By August 1853 the shabby courthouse had been demolished, and the work on the proposed structure begun, but there were the usual delays and cost overruns associated with public building projects. However, the citizens were so pleased with the building that the extra funds were willingly allocated.

Built in that rustic classicism so popular from Maine to Florida before the Civil War, the severity of its Doric porch was relieved with touches of whimsy, including the town clock from old St. Paul's church embedded in its pediment, water spouts that looked more like the pigs that once roamed the streets than the lions in Ellison's design, and a cupola perched on its roof to aid in the detection of fires. The brick work of this temple of justice was stuccoed, then colored and scored to resemble yellow sandstone. Thus by the middle of the decade Lynchburg had a new courthouse worthy of the nation's second wealthiest city, gas for illumination like New York or Philadelphia, its first real sewer on Market Street, and a college.

Of all the calamities that occurred in the city during the Civil War, the tale of the first Lynchburg College is perhaps the most poignant. The founders of the antebellum Madison College in Uniontown, Pennsylvania, had tried to promote harmony and understanding among the several sections of the United States in a most singular way. Many of the members of the faculty of this Methodist school and its student body were recruited from the South. Until the debate over slavery became more strident, this unique experiment seemed to work well. However, by 1850, apprehensive that the students were being exposed to a steady diet of abolitionist propaganda, many parents forced their sons to transfer to Southern colleges and universities.

Finally, in 1855, when rumors of the possibility of racial integration at Madison College reached the faculty, a number of professors decided to leave Uniontown and found a college below the Mason-Dixon Line. Lynchburg was chosen as the location of the first Methodist Episcopal college for men in the South because it was blessed with a salubrious climate, an excellent system of public transportation, and a generous, supportive citizenry.

A generation earlier, the townsfolk had hoped that Thomas Jefferson might have chosen Lynchburg as the site of the University of Virginia. The placement of that institution in Charlottesville was a blow to civic pride, but now, with its own college, Lynchburg could forget its disappointment and look forward to becoming a seat of learning.

The first session began on October 1, 1855, with a faculty of five and a student body of 81, 50 of whom were from the Lynchburg area. Classes that first year were held in a building on the corner of Fifth and Clay Streets, the site of the future Biggers Elementary School. The faculty and the boarding students occupied lodging in a house at the corner of Sixth and Court Streets, just a short walk from their classroom building. Thanks to the success of the college's first fund drive, these arrangements proved temporary. Soon on a square bounded by Tenth, Floyd, Eleventh, and

LYNCHBURG

Wise Streets the foundation was laid for the structures that would give this part of Lynchburg its name—College Hill. Described as "military" Gothic, they resembled the buildings that housed Virginia Military Institute in Lexington, Virginia.

The curriculum was traditional, with an emphasis on the classics. The contention that Greek and Latin literature gave support to the institution of slavery is not correct; the opposite view could as equally be accurate. The similar thesis that the study of modern history might encourage impressionable students to become revolutionaries is likewise ridiculous. Any quantity of information may be shaped by a skillful teacher into any world view. Actually, the course of study adopted by the faculty of the first Lynchburg College, like that of its namesake half a century later, was almost universally regarded as forming the basis of a sound formal education. Useful subjects were mastered in trade schools or in the work place. Until the early twentieth century, a similar pattern of instruction based on that of the English universities Oxford and Cambridge predominated in American higher education.

The most controversial aspect of life at Lynchburg College was the military character of the discipline administered by the faculty. The fact that many colleges employed military training and uniforms did not diminish the antipathy of the Methodist Church to such instruction on a campus with a strong religious affiliation. In the beginning military education was voluntary, with parental permission for boys over the age of fourteen, but as the tensions between the North and the South increased, it was made compulsory.

The first class graduated in 1856, ending a very successful year. A 25 percent increase in the student body and a generous endowment from the City of Lynchburg indicated a bright future for the new college. With a 40-member board in place and a charter granted by the State of Virginia in 1858, the administration launched a program of expansion that included the sale of perpetual scholarships. For $500 ($8,715 in 2000) one could buy a scholarship that could be passed from one generation to another.

Equally popular was the college's annual Speech Day, when each class of graduates was honored. This was a regular feature of academic life on many campuses. In 1856 the tone was light-hearted, but as the years passed, the tension of national events intruded into the orations, and by the spring of 1861, when the sixth and final session ended, graduation was a somber event. That summer many of the students and faculty marched off to war, and the use of the buildings as a college passed into history.

During the War the college was transformed into a hospital, a function for which it was well suited, but at the end of that conflict in April 1865 it was converted into Union barracks during the occupation of Lynchburg. Well maintained by Confederate medical personnel, the buildings were plundered by Federal soldiers and left fit to only provide shelter for the homeless.

Between 1868 and 1872, the Lynchburg Classical and Commercial School found a home amid the slowly crumbling halls of Lynchburg College, but that venture was short lived; before the century ended much of the material and the fixtures had been incorporated into other buildings. Only two of the original structures still stood: 1300 Tenth Street and 1301 Eleventh Street. They were preserved as private dwellings until they too were demolished in the 1960s.

The existence of the first Lynchburg College is marked with a bronze memorial plaque in the Hall Campus Center at the second Lynchburg College.

IN COMMEMORATION

OF

THE FIRST LYNCHBURG COLLEGE

THE FACULTY AND THE STUDENTS

1855-1861

While the present and the initial Lynchburg Colleges

have separate and distinct histories, we want to

honor the nineteenth-century college for its

contributions to higher education in

Central Virginia.

Erected By

The Old Dominion Chapter

of

The United Daughters of the Confederacy

April 2000

Lynchburg often receives its first winter storm close to the feast of the Epiphany; in 1856 it fell on January 8. However, even a foot or two of snow could not dampen the spirits of the citizens; the Virginia and Tennessee Railway was close to its ultimate goal. Despite snow, rain, and summer heat the crews laid mile after mile of track, and on October 1 the line was finished to Bristol and the first train made its journey. Central and southwestern Virginia were finally linked.

1856 was an election year, but the replacement of the lackluster Franklin Pierce by the ineffectual James Buchanan invoked little interest in Lynchburg. Members of the legal community and the average resident were more interested in a case that was in its last stages before the Supreme Court. Born in bondage in Missouri, Dred

Scott had been taken to the Wisconsin Territory by his owner in the 1830s. When his master died, Scott sued for his freedom based on the provisions of the Northwest Ordinance of 1787 and the Missouri Compromise. He was set free, but the Missouri Supreme Court overturned the decision and reduced Scott to slavery again in 1852. Scott's new owner moved to New York, but left him in Missouri. He now sued for his freedom in a federal court, and the case was heard by the Supreme Court in 1856.

Shortly after Buchanan's inauguration in March 1857, Chief Justice Roger B. Taney announced the court's decision. Scott was still a slave and could not sue for his freedom. Blacks, regardless of their previous, current, or future status, could not be citizens. The Missouri Compromise of 1820 was unconstitutional, and thus Congress could not prohibit slavery in the territories. *Dred Scott v. Stanford* was enthusiastically greeted in Lynchburg as a vindication of the institution of slavery, but it gave the Republican Party another cause they could exploit in future elections. Their candidate in the recent contest, John C. Frémont, had run a strong second to the victorious Buchanan. As the national economy slid into a recession they found still another issue to utilize.

Foreign gold and silver coins were accepted as legal tender in the United States from the early days of the Republic until the passage of the act of February 21, 1857, which demonetized them. Each merchant had a set of scales and tools to weigh and test foreign bullion. The exchange of foreign coins for domestic pieces—the new small copper-nickel cent and silver coinage—continued until June 25, 1860.

This change in the monetary system only aggravated the Panic of 1857, which led to a severe nationwide economic slump in October. Luckily the financial collapse seems not to have affected Lynchburg as much as it did other cities of comparable size. Lynchburg's dependence on one commodity might have in time proved a potential disaster, but in 1857 public demand for chewing tobacco maintained the city's healthy economic growth. The Republicans made use of the Panic of 1857 to advance their economic plan for recovery that included a protective tariff, federal aid for internal improvements, and free 160-acre homesteads to settlers on public lands, including immigrants. They were slowly building a winning coalition that would cross social and economic lines.

On October 18, 1859, news reached Lynchburg of John Brown's raid on Harper's Ferry. It seemed to fulfill the hopes or fears of every segment of the population. Was this the beginning of the long-feared slave rebellion, or the end of national unity? Captured by Colonel Robert E. Lee, a hero of the Mexican War, Brown was convicted of murder on October 31. When he was hanged on December 2, 1859, tensions momentarily eased. However, by then Lynchburgers had already begun planning for their own defense.

On November 8, the Home Guard was organized with Samuel Garland Jr. as captain. The next day, other military companies were formed: the 131st Virginia Militia under Colonel W.B. Brown, the Wise Volunteer Troop with Captain Caelton Radford, the Rifle Guards under Captain M.S. Langhorne, the Lynchburg Infantry Grays under Captain A.F. Biggers, and the Artillery under Captain John Shields. Three weeks later on Wednesday, November 30, a meeting was held at Martin's Warehouse to discuss the city's possible response to the North. Local paranoia had reached the point that it was assumed an attack was imminent. However, there was still time to save the Union, and there were men and women in Lynchburg brave enough to try and counter the madness about to consume the nation.

There was an almost frantic quality to the holiday season of 1859–1860 among the affluent, but for the less fortunate it was quite different. In 1852, Harriet Beecher Stowe published her then controversial novel, *Uncle Toms Cabin*, or *Life Among the Lowly*. The latter part of its title might also have easily applied to the poorer white citizens of Lynchburg. Theirs was a precarious existence, wholly dependent on the ability of each individual to earn a living. Illiterate and often devoid of any marketable skills, they worked for pitiful wages. Slaves rarely performed tasks that might put them in risk of serious injury or death; they were, after all, valuable pieces of property. Such tasks were reserved for poor whites, and particularly Irish immigrants who had been arriving in central Virginia in ever-increasing numbers since the 1840s. The death or injury of the breadwinner in a poor family could spell disaster. Private charity often meant the difference between starvation and survival, but it was not distributed evenly.

While most philanthropy was motivated by a genuine sense of Christian obligation, in some cases it was a form of social control. Those who dispensed gifts of food and clothing to Lynchburg's poor might not be familiar with David Ricardo's *Principles of Political Economy and Taxation*, published in 1817, but they certainly agreed with his "iron law of wages:" pay the poor more than subsistence wages and they will only spend the excess on liquor and producing more children. In the view of many middle class citizens, poverty was the end result of idleness and a total absence of initiative. The poor were destitute because they wanted to be that way. In such a climate of indifference, petty crime and prostitution were often the only choices for some of the destitute.

On the south side of Jefferson Street, to the junction of Horseford Road, was a row of dilapidated frame buildings known collectively as Buzzards' Roost, or simply the Buzzard. This cluster of shanties housed the taverns, gambling dens, and bordellos that gave the waterfront district of Lynchburg such an unsavory reputation. While the police kept track of the activities in the area, few arrests were made, and even fewer convictions for prostitution, public drunkenness, or disturbing the peace. The area was considered a necessary evil, a safety valve for the city's poor. There were establishments catering to white patrons, and those that were exclusively for black customers, both slave and free. Alcohol was cheap and available in a number of forms, but beer and whiskey were preferred. For their services, prostitutes charged from 50¢ in working class houses to $10 in the establishments catering to the needs of wealthy clients.

With the arrival of the railways and the increase in travelers to the Hill City, the "traffic in vice" expanded. However, the races did not mix even in the enjoyment of their pleasures. As a rule poor whites supported legal bondage, not because they ever hoped to own slaves, but because it provided them with a permanent inferior class beneath them.

In the future when those who survived the war looked back on the last full year of peace, the only really happy event they could remember occurred on January 14 when the first train from the Orange and Alexandria Railroad reached the Amherst side of the James River. Passengers were conveyed to and from the Virginia and Tennessee depot to the new terminus in omnibuses known as "Latham's coaches." The arrival of another rail line was the harbinger of an even brighter future. However, the organization on May 8 of yet another military unit, the Lynchburg Mechanics' Artillery with Captain H. Grey Latham, was an intimation for some that the city's prospects might not be so promising after all.

On Saturday, June 23, the unthinkable occurred. There was a shootout at the corner of Twelfth and Church Streets involving Charles, George, Robert, and Joseph Button of the *Virginian*, Lynchburg's pro Whig paper, and George and William Hardwicke of the pro Democratic *Republican* paper. Charles Button had assumed the editorship of the *Virginian* in April 1857, and his biting wit and sarcasm had irritated a number of his fellow citizens. That day his brother Joseph was killed and Robert was severely wounded. George Hardwicke was arrested and brought to trial for murder, but he was acquitted. William was not charged. It was indicative of the underlying tensions that were about to tear the city apart.

In the fall, citizens of Lynchburg were caught up in the presidential election. The Democrats nominated Stephen A. Douglas and H.V. Johnson, while the Constitutional Union Party chose John Bell of Tennessee and Edward Everett of Massachusetts. Everett had spoken in favor of the Union to an enthusiastic crowd when he visited Lynchburg on May 4, 1858. The Secessionists nominated then Vice-President John C. Breckinridge of Kentucky and Senator Joseph Lane of Oregon, while the Republicans nominated Abraham Lincoln of Illinois and Hannibal Hamlin of Maine, a former Jacksonian Democrat. However, the Republican ticket did not appear on the ballot in Virginia.

Lynchburg's vote was: Bell 969, Breckinridge 487, and Douglas 132. In 1860 there were 18 free states and 15 slave states. Breckinridge carried every cotton state as well as North Carolina, Maryland, and Delaware. Virginia, Kentucky, and Tennessee went for Bell. Douglas carried only Missouri, and Lincoln took every free state giving him 1,866,452 popular votes and 180 electoral votes. Douglas polled 1,376,957 but received only 12 electoral votes; Although Breckinridge received only 849,781 popular votes, he was awarded 72 electoral votes. In popular votes, Bell was last with 588,879, but he received 39 electoral votes. Bell had sought the middle course of moderation—the Constitution, the Union, and law enforcement—with reason and compromise. The response of the forces of secession to Lincoln's election were swift. On December 20, South Carolina passed the ordinance of secession. Seven days later Federal troops at Fort Moultrie were evacuated to Fort Sumter. Fort Moultrie was burned. For many this was the first act of war against the government of the United States.

In response to President Buchanan's proclamation that January 4 would be a national day of prayer and fasting for peace, services were held in a number of Lynchburg churches. But events were moving too swiftly for those who knelt in the winter twilight and begged for deliverance. On February 2, when Lynchburg chose her delegates to the state convention to be held in Richmond starting on February 14, the voters courageously selected men who favored the preservation of the Union. Abraham Lincoln was inaugurated as President of the United States on March 21 and offered sincere conciliation and possible mediation to those who were rending the nation.

On April 4, 1861, the Virginia Convention voted against secession. Then, early on the morning of Friday, April 12, Edmund Ruffin fired the first shot on Fort Sumter. Time was running out for the Federal garrison, and for the Commonwealth of Virginia. On April 15, President Lincoln called for 75,000 volunteers; Virginia's share was to be 2,340. After an agonizing two-day session, the Virginia Convention reversed its previous decision and voted to secede. It was April 17, 1861.

Eighty years had passed since the end of the American Revolution, and Virginians had forgotten how terrible war could be. The War of 1812 had been brief and its main engagements far from central Virginia. The Mexican War had been fought by professionals, and transformed into an adventure by the nation's newspapers. The horrors of the Crimean War had occurred half a world away, and Alfred Lord Tennyson's 1854 poem, "The Charge of the Light Brigade," romanticized a needless slaughter for his British and American readers. Now for the first time the citizens of Lynchburg would experience the privation, the pain, the horrible loss associated with armed conflict; and this was the most unfortunate of all struggles because it was to be a civil war—father against son, brother against brother, American against American. The nation that Virginia's sons and daughters had sacrificed their lives and sacred fortunes to create in 1776 would be forever changed. Likewise, Lynchburg would never be the same again. At the dawn of Lynchburg's "Golden Decade" one enthusiastic writer had predicted that the city would soon become "the metropolis of Southwest Virginia;" sadly, that title was reserved for Roanoke, whose genesis lay in the post–war period.

Chapter Five

"RICH MAN'S WAR, POOR MAN'S FIGHT" 1861–1865

The conflict between 1861 and 1865 that almost destroyed the United States is known by many names, but to the residents of Lynchburg it is simply "the War." Six generations have passed since Lee surrendered at Appomattox, and the veil of memory has softened the remembrance of the suffering and privation. Only the myths and romance remain. Today, all over the United States the descendants of "Johnny Reb" and "Billy Yank" spend enormous sums to recreate the uniforms and accoutrements used by their ancestors so they can reproduce those moments in time when the fate of the Republic hung in the balance. When the mock combats are done, they leave the field of battle for good fellowship; but can they ever know the horror, sense of loss, and the hopelessness of those they seek to honor?

When the students at Lynchburg College raised a Confederate flag on April 6, 1861, it was not a boyish prank, but a shadow of things to come. Within days the Stars and Stripes had vanished, and the Virginia state flag had taken its place. On Tuesday, April 23, the first Lynchburg soldiers to leave for Richmond were given a solemn farewell. The streets leading to the Southside depot were lined with men, women, and children, white and black, slave and free. At the intersection of Main and Bridge Streets (now Main and Ninth) the ardent secessionist Reverend Mr. Jacob Duche Mitchell of the Second Presbyterian Church (now Westminster Presbyterian Church) delivered the invocation and reminded these soldiers untested in battle why they were fighting and risking death. They were defending their homes and families against "the enemy." The men were loaded in freight cars without ventilation, the prime mode of troop transport during the war, but they soon knocked holes in the sides.

Lynchburg would field a total of 12 companies during the war in addition to the Silver Grays, composed of men over 45 and charged with keeping public order. Most soldiers were able to supply their own uniforms and their personal kit; the women of Lynchburg provided these necessities for the poorer soldiers. Thus between 1861 and 1865 approximately 80 percent of the white male population of the city would see service in a branch of the Confederate armed forces. About a fifth were wounded or died from various causes, close to a fifth were captured, but only a fifth of the veterans were mustered out of the military at the end of the war. What was the fate of the remaining forty percent? Some acquired substitutes—a practice common on both sides of the conflict—until it was forbidden by law in the Confederacy on December 28, 1863. Others defected to the Union Army, but the majority simply returned home, unaware of the fact that separation from the services required a formal discharge. As the hopelessness of the Confederate cause became painfully apparent, many men obviously felt a greater concern for their families than an abstraction. Such behavior had been a problem during the various colonial wars, as well as the American Revolution. General George Washington had seen his army wax and wane with the seasons as recruits returned home to plant or harvest.

It is unlikely that most of these men who were being asked to offer up their lives for "the Cause" had more than a vague understanding of states rights, or the Hamiltonian vision of an America built on commerce and industry versus the Jeffersonian dream of an agrarian republic of independent farmers. For some that day of parting was the beginning of a modern adventure straight from the pages of a novel by Sir Walter Scott; for others it marked an escape from an existence with little promise. In time they would all experience the grim realities of war, but on that bright spring morning thoughts of death and defeat were probably far from their minds.

Most of them did not own slaves and simply accepted involuntary servitude as part of the natural order of things; after all, the entire Bible was filled with references to slavery. However, the Federal forces would quickly gain the moral high ground by making emancipation a rallying cry in those states that remained within the Union. The same comparison may be drawn between the Southern song, "The Bonnie Blue Flag," with its rather vague references to concepts and ideas, and the very specific agenda outlined in Julia Ward Howe's "The Battle Hymn of the Republic." The North gained the edge in the propaganda war, and never lost it.

On May 23, 1861, the voters of Lynchburg approved by unanimous consent the Virginia ordinance of secession. No sooner had the Old Dominion left the Union than coins in all denominations, but particularly silver and gold, began to disappear from circulation into dresser drawers, strong boxes, and other hiding places. They would reappear after the war, but in 1861 they were regarded as a hedge against inflation and economic privation. There were three branches of the United States Mint in the South (Charlotte, North Carolina; Dahlonega, Georgia; and New Orleans, Louisiana), but a shortage of bullion made a Confederate coinage unfeasible.

Robert Lovett Jr., an engraver and die sinker from Philadelphia, produced dies for a small cent to be struck in copper-nickel in 1861, but he was afraid that he might be arrested and charged with treason if he delivered the dies. They remained hidden in his basement until after the war. Thus the Confederate States of America were forced to rely on a paper currency for fractional denominations as well as multiples of the dollar. They inflated throughout the conflict until they were not worth the paper on which they were printed; thus those citizens of Lynchburg who invested in Confederate currency and bonds lost their money. It is ironic that in the twenty-first century collectors pay premium prices for these faded scraps of nineteenth-century paper.

Lynchburg was a garrison city during the war because of its three rail lines; however, they also made it a prime target for the enemy. Prices soared and resources were strained or depleted as 10,000 soldiers almost overwhelmed a population of 6,800 during the months that followed secession. Because Lynchburg was not prepared for such a large influx of troops, those not from Virginia were bivouacked in inadequate makeshift shelters at the Fair Grounds, now Miller Park, while Virginians were assigned to Camp Davis, a wooded area bounded by the modern Kemper, Pierce, Twelfth, and Sixteenth Streets. Lack of sanitation in these two camps provided a breeding ground for a whole host of communicable diseases from smallpox to diarrhea.

Thus Lynchburg soon became a hospital center. Lynchburg College, the General Military Hospital, under the direction of Dr. Henry Grey Latham, was the first. Dr. William Otway Owen was his senior surgeon. Before the end of the war there would be eight hospitals in Lynchburg, as well as a special facility at the Pest House for smallpox cases. Those who died in Lynchburg during the war were buried by George A. Diuguid, who operated the second oldest mortuary in the United States, which he founded in 1817. In 1861 one could choose either a metallic or wooden coffin, but as metal grew scarce, wood became the only choice. By the end of the war a shroud was all that was available for some burials. When embalming became impossible because of a lack of proper supplies, bodies were packed in charcoal to be shipped to grieving families both above and below the Mason-Dixon Line.

Troops from other parts of the Confederacy poured into Lynchburg all through the summer. Many of these recruits had never been far from home, and they took the opportunity to behave in a manner that was not condoned in polite society. Saloons, gambling dens, and bordellos did a thriving business. Drunken soldiers roamed the streets at night, brawling with each other as well as with citizens. Lynchburg's streets were no longer safe, and neither the Silver Grays or the local police could keep order.

Between July 18 and 21, troops from Lynchburg were involved in the Battle of First Manassas, and shortly thereafter the wounded began to arrive. It soon became obvious that Lynchburg needed another hospital, and Mrs. Lucy Minor Otey was equally determined to provide it—Dr. Owen was determined that she would not.

Mrs. Otey went to Richmond and gained permission from President Jefferson Davis to organize and supervise the Ladies Relief Hospital Association. He also granted her the rank of Captain. When the Ladies Relief Hospital was recognized by the Confederate government on October 13, it was granted government rations. The new hospital was located in the City Hotel, formerly the Union Hotel, on the northeast corner of Sixth and Main Streets, and Dr. Thomas L. Walker was the chief surgeon. It became the most popular hospital among the wounded because, in the tradition of Florence Nightingale, it was a cleaner and better managed facility.

Paper in 1861 had a high rag content, and the best quality line was produced in the mills of Pennsylvania. When it was no longer available and every scrap of cloth was needed for clothing or bandages, the city's two newspapers had to curtail their publication schedules, but they continued to produce their journals until the last days of the war. The technology for producing cheaper paper made with wood pulp would not be perfected until a decade after the war ended.

The continued presence of so many soldiers in Lynchburg was a constant drain on the resources of the city, and by the end of 1861 everything seemed in short supply. In the letters, papers, and memoirs of the Blackford family there is a rich source of first hand impressions of the war and its effect on the citizens of Lynchburg.

Typhoid fever was a constant threat, and rumors of smallpox struck fear into soldier and civilian alike. It was a highly contagious disease and those in the prime of life seemed particularly susceptible. Vaccination in various forms against smallpox had been known and practiced since the early eighteenth century, but children—particularly in rural areas—were not routinely protected against it, and many of the soldiers who passed through Lynchburg were farm bred. Luckily the first actual case was not diagnosed until October 1862, almost a year later. Dr. John Jay Terrell set up a smallpox hospital at the Pest House near the Methodist Cemetery.

The devotion of the women of Lynchburg to the needs of the sick and dying was phenomenal, and the commitment of the Roman Catholic Sisters of Charity was exceptional. Without hesitation, they exposed themselves to every danger; they were the only nurses willing to tend to the smallpox victims. With their help, Dr. Terrell prevented an epidemic and saved the lives of most of his patients. The only clergyman willing to risk his life and minister to the spiritual needs of the smallpox victims was Father Louis-Hippolyte Gache; the Reverend Mr. Mitchell might roam the wards of the hospitals exhorting the sick and dying to repent, but neither he nor his fellow clergymen ventured near the Pest House.

The women of Buzzard's Roost also made their offerings to the war effort. To each and every fund drive they gave discreet contributions through third parties. Whether these were given because of a sense of patriotism and civic pride, or in the hope of influencing their status in the next life is not known, but until the disappearance of these women from the life of Lynchburg in the 1950s they seldom failed to answer the call of charity. However, their often generous donations were always anonymous.

By the end of 1861, a limited system of bartering was being used in the city. As fuel became scarce, merchants gladly accepted firewood or coal in place of currency. The first Christmas of the war passed and the new year began with the false hope that the conflict might end soon and all the soldiers would leave. Unfortunately, matters only grew worse. Mayor William Branch forbade the sale of liquor, but his feeble effort at temperance failed. Some called for martial law to be imposed in the city, but that did not happen. Finally, in August 1862 the Confederate government established a provost guard in Lynchburg, and his discipline and careful supervision of the troops helped to improve the situation.

In the spring of 1862, Lynchburg's hospitals were taxed almost beyond their limits with wounded pouring into the city from Stonewall Jackson's campaign in the Shenandoah Valley as well as the Peninsula Campaign. There were so many wounded that citizens took some of the less serious cases into their homes. Even this was not enough; often patients whose wounds were not life-threatening would be treated and then placed on the floor on pallets wherever there was space. As the months passed and casualties increased, trains would arrive during the night and simply leave the wounded on the platforms where at first light those who were still alive would be discovered and taken to one of the hospitals. However, when soldiers from Lynchburg were wounded or killed, local citizens risked their lives to bring them home for care or burial.

On Sunday, September 14, 1862, Brigadier General Samuel Garland was killed in Boonsboro, Maryland, during General Lee's incursion into northern-held territory. He was brought home and buried on Friday, September 19. Garland seems to have been one of the civilians who stepped into the military life and made a success of it. The existence of companies in the Civil War on both sides followed a long-established pattern. Men of substance would raise a company, design the uniforms, and outfit the recruits from their own resources. Many of these "gentlemen soldiers" were unfit to command anyone, and often the survival of their men depended on the non-commissioned officers. The only deviation from this pattern occurred in the French army during the wars of the Revolution and Napoleon, when command and promotion were based on talent alone. Who knows how many men of the quality of Napoleon's greatest commanders—Lannes, Murat, Masséna, and Ney—were trapped in the ranks without the chance to show their true talents. Throughout the war there was a great deal of tension between commanders and subordinates, and sometimes it would erupt into violence. Samuel Garland seems to have had the respect as well as the love of his men, and they sincerely mourned his untimely death.

Lynchburg was not only a garrison city; on June 10, 1862, over 3,000 Union prisoners began to arrive. They remained at the Fair Grounds until August when they were transferred to Richmond. When the canal was damaged by spring flooding they actually helped repair it, but did cause some trouble for their hosts by introducing counterfeit bills into circulation. Seven months later on January 15, 1863, 1,000 more Federal prisoners arrived from Murfreesboro, Tennessee. The authorities were not ready for them, so these miserable captives were held in the open in the bitter cold, in a cordoned area of Main and Church, until they could be transferred to the Fair Grounds.

On January 1, 1863, President Lincoln issued the Emancipation Proclamation. Technically it freed the slaves in the states that were in rebellion against the Union, but while it certainly gave those in bondage hope, as the news began to filter through the channels providing escape through the Underground Railroad "stations" in the Lynchburg area, few gained their freedom. By 1863, many Lynchburg residents were forced to sell their personal possessions at auction, including their remaining slaves, simply to maintain a minimum standard of living. It seemed that every day brought another disappointment, and every week another crisis. Then the unthinkable occurred.

On May 10, Stonewall Jackson was mortally wounded at Chancellorsville, and three days later his body arrived in Lynchburg on its way to Lexington for burial. As his remains were placed on the packet boat *John Marshall* for the journey home, the white citizens of Lynchburg turned out in droves to pay their respects to the man who might have saved the Confederacy. As the wounded from the same battle that claimed Jackson's life poured into Lynchburg, a critical shortage developed in the supply of useable bandages. Everything was commandeered for this purpose, including bed clothes, table linens; any piece of serviceable cloth was donated to the hospitals, even the linings of draperies and ladies' petticoats.

The news of the fall of Vicksburg on July 3, 1863, and the defeat at Gettysburg on July 4, were bitter reverses, but they forced the citizens of Lynchburg to face the possibility of a local attack. For the remainder of the year their energies were devoted to strengthening the city's defenses. A warning system was created, including a constant watch of all possible entry routes to the city. Everyone including able-bodied slaves and the walking wounded were pressed into service building fortifications at every anticipated point of incursion.

"Rich Man's War, Poor Man's Fight": 1861–1865

The winter of 1863–1864 saw a series of devastating fires that were deliberately set, but the arsonists were never apprehended. In the minds of some, this carefully planned destruction of property and critical stores was the work of the "Heroes of America," a secret antiwar society composed of Unionists in the military and civilian population. However, this widely held suspicion was never proved. The citizens suffered another disappointment on January 14 when a meeting was held in the hope of moving Randolph-Macon College from Mecklenburg County to the safer location of Lynchburg. A decade earlier the city had easily funded the founding of Lynchburg College, but adequate funds were completely lacking, even in inflated bonds and currency.

The dwindling resources of the city had to be devoted to the war effort. By March 1, 1864, there were 4,000 wounded soldiers in Lynchburg hospitals. Doctors were forced to amputate and operate without basic painkilling supplies. Then early in June the news that citizens had feared for months was confirmed. On June 6, 1864, General Grant ordered General David Hunter, who was in command of the Department of West Virginia, to advance on Lynchburg and take it and destroy the rail lines around the city.

Hunter was in Staunton, and on June 9, he approved General William W. Averell's plan for taking Lynchburg. The following day, the Union army began to move south because speed was absolutely essential for the strategy to succeed. With limited resources, General John McCausland was able to slow the Federal advance, and after the first day the Federals had only reached a point within 10 miles of Lexington. On June 11, they entered that city with little difficulty. By telegraph, the citizens of Lynchburg received the news of Lexington's fall and knew they were next.

According to Averell's plan, General Alfred Duffie was to cross the James River after destroying the military stores at Amherst Court House and dismantle enough of the Southside railway to prevent it from being used to reinforce Lynchburg. General Hunter had a reputation for destroying everything in his path; the rumor sweeping through Central Virginia incorrectly claimed that he had burned all of Lexington. It was assumed that Duffie would do likewise, and so residents of Amherst County began to seek shelter in Lynchburg. But as Duffie approached his objective, Hunter recalled him to Lexington. He had no choice but to obey orders and on June 13, rejoined his commander. The limited damage Duffie had done to the Orange and Alexandria railroad was easily repaired. Hunter's fatal mistake was remaining in Lexington until the fourteenth; he should have left for Lynchburg a day earlier.

As Hunter headed south, General Jubal A. Early moved towards Charlottesville from Richmond, and General John C. Breckinridge, still suffering from an injury received at the battle of Cold Harbor, rushed towards the beleaguered city, reaching it on June 15. He collapsed and was placed under medical observation. By this time the Union army had reached the town of Liberty (now Bedford). Soon Hunter began to receive conflicting reports on the defenses of Lynchburg. Once again he hesitated. Meanwhile, Early was moving south from Charlottesville via the Orange and Alexandria railroad.

On June 16, General Hunter advanced on Lynchburg, reaching New London by nightfall. Here he received intelligence that Lynchburg's defenses on the western edge were barely manned. On the morning of June 17, Hunter inched forward as Early moved rapidly southward, arriving in Lynchburg in the afternoon. As the day passed, the Federals probed the perimeter of the city, and there were a series of brief skirmishes lasting until nightfall. Among Hunter's officers in the Lynchburg campaign were two future American presidents, Colonel Rutherford B. Hayes and Major William McKinley.

Hunter made his headquarters at Sandusky House, the home of retired Army paymaster Major George C. Hutter, whom Hunter had known before the war. That night Hunter learned with disbelief that Lynchburg had been reinforced. It was then that one of the most ingenious events associated with the deliverance of Lynchburg occurred. General Early, or "Old Jube" as his soldiers loved to call him, ordered that during the night an empty train be run up and down the tracks of the Southside Railroad over the old Tin Bridge. Built of wood, the bridge was covered with metal to protect it from rotting, but the residents in the immediate vicinity considered it a public nuisance. Every time a train crossed it, the sound produced could wake a person from a deep sleep. Combined with shouting and the constant blowing of the train's whistle, Hunter was convinced that the Confederate army intended to defend the city no matter what the cost.

On the morning of June 18, 16,000 Confederates faced 19,000 Federals, and anxious citizens milled about the streets listening to the sounds of battle drifting like distant thunder from the west. Some had even packed their valuables with the intention of fleeing across the river if the Union army breached Lynchburg's inner defenses. Convinced Hunter would sack the city, some merchants pitched their goods into the streets and urged the passersby to help themselves before the Yankees stole everything that they did not burn. By the afternoon more Confederate reinforcements under General Robert E. Rodes and General John D. Gordon arrived from Charlottesville, tipping the balance against the Federals. By evening, Hunter had evacuated his headquarters, resolving to retreat towards Liberty, which he reached by forced march at dawn on June 19. Lynchburg had survived.

"Rich Man's War, Poor Man's Fight": 1861–1865

General John McCausland was given a sword and a pair of silver spurs that cost $3,000 in Confederate currency, or $100 in United States coin, for his part in delivering Lynchburg in her hour of need. As General Early pursued Hunter, he sent a flood of prisoners to Lynchburg, where they quickly taxed the facilities set aside for Union soldiers. Answering the city's appeal, the Confederate government ordered all prisoners in Lynchburg and Richmond to the infamous Camp Andersonville in Sumter, Georgia.

At the Battle of Winchester on September 19, Early finally encountered stiff resistance from Union forces, and among the casualties was one of the heroes of the Battle of Lynchburg, General Robert Emmett Rodes. A year earlier the citizens had gathered to mourn the death of another native son, Samuel Garland; now it was the turn of Robert Rodes. His funeral and Masonic service were held on Friday, September 23, with burial in the Presbyterian Cemetery. The burial grounds inside and outside the city were quickly filling with the best of a lost generation.

By the fall of 1864, boys of 17 were conscripted into the army, along with every other male in good health. Slaves were forced to work on fortifications and provide auxiliary services. Poor families were particularly hard hit when the breadwinner was drafted, but unfortunately private charity was no longer able to supplement the needs of the less fortunate. Each day brought news of new casualties and more and more slaves escaping to the Union lines. Their future above the Mason-Dixon Line was uncertain, but at least they were free at last.

There were two serious unsolved fires in the fall of 1864, which destroyed stores as well as dwellings. The rumors of a year earlier re-emerged, and names of suspects were passed from one gossip to another, but nothing was ever proved. With fuel and food shortages, the holiday season was bleak indeed. Hoarding had been a problem since the war began, and while it was condemned in the press and from the pulpit it continued beyond the end of the conflict. Merchants were often the focus of public anger. They were regularly accused, for the most part unjustly, of forcing up prices for their own benefit. Some merchants actually lost their businesses trying to provide continued regular service to their customers during wartime. The extension of credit, even on a limited basis, to clients who were unable to pay because of the absence or death of the breadwinner proved disastrous to many businessmen.

On February 28, 1865, a public meeting was held to discuss the possibility of surrendering the city to the Union forces in the area. It would mean the removal of the Confederate wounded from Lynchburg and a subsequent easing of shortages of food and fuel. The federal government would supposedly supply the citizens' basic needs until the end of hostilities, but they would be under military rule. The debate lasted until after midnight, but it was finally resolved by voting to continue the struggle.

LYNCHBURG

Within hours of this decision the rumor reached the city that General Philip H. Sheridan was approaching Lynchburg. Stripped of most of its able-bodied males, its troops, and with its crumbling defenses unmanned, there was panic in the city. Luckily, Sheridan headed towards Petersburg, never aware that he might have taken the city without a fight. On March 24, the *Virginian* ceased publication; the *Lynchburg Republican* had already stopped its press for lack of supplies. There were rumors that Richmond had fallen and Lee was heading westward towards Lynchburg. On April 6, state officials began to arrive via the canal. Lynchburg was to briefly become the capital of Virginia, and it was feared that the last battle of the war might be fought on the hills above the James.

As Lee moved towards Lynchburg he was trapped by Grant at Appomattox, and on April 9, Palm Sunday, the end came quietly in the parlor of Wilbur McLean. When the news reached Lynchburg later that day, the troops immediately began to vacate the city. Only those servicemen who were too sick to move were left. An almost deathly quiet settled over the Fair Grounds and Camp Davis. Some believed that the Union forces would burn Lynchburg, but in fact it would be the only major city in Virginia to be physically untouched by the war.

It was with some trepidation that Mayor Branch handed over control of the city to Union General Ranald S. Mackensie at the entrance to Lynchburg on the bridge over the canal at Horseford Road on the morning of Wednesday, April 12, 1865. Civil order was quickly restored, and the Federal force remained in the city until Monday, April 17. There were some problems with the newly freed slaves, but the Federal soldiers and the free black community quickly brought the situation under control. On Good Friday, April 14, Lynchburgers learned of the assassination of President Lincoln, an event greeted with foreboding. Easter that year was a somber event as Northerners and Southerners filled the churches of Lynchburg to mark the end of the war and the beginning of the ecclesiastical year. The future was already grim; now it was also frighteningly uncertain.

A lean-to in the Monacan village at Natural Bridge, Virginia, 2003. (Dorothy Potter.)

Reproduction of a Monacan dwelling in the Monacan village at Natural Bridge, Virginia, 2003. (Dorothy Potter.)

The Miller Claytor House at the corner of 8th and Church Streets. (Jones Memorial Library.)

The oldest known public announcement (1818) of an amateur theater production in Lynchburg. (Lynchburg Press.)

By the Lynchburg Thespian
SOCIETY.

ON Tuesday evening the 8th of December next, (In Messrs. J. & P. Labby's Brick Building, back of Messrs. A. Robinson & Co's. Store) will be presented

GODWINS Celebrated
Tragedy of
ANTONIO,

To which will be added the Farce of

" How to Die for Love."

Tickets to be had at the Book Store of Messrs. Ward & Digges. Doors to be opened at 6 and Curtains to rise at 7 o'clock precisely. Admittance one dollar.

November 30. ‡3t21

Panoramic view of Lynchburg, 1855. Artist Edward Beyer created similar illustrations of a number of American antebellum communities. (Jones Memorial Library.)

Packetboat on the James River and Kanawha Canal, 1850. (Jones Memorial Library.)

An ox cart in antebellum Lynchburg, 1860. (Sesquicentennial Committee.)

The Old City Market House between Main and Church Streets, with the courthouse in the background, 1859. (Jones Memorial Library.)

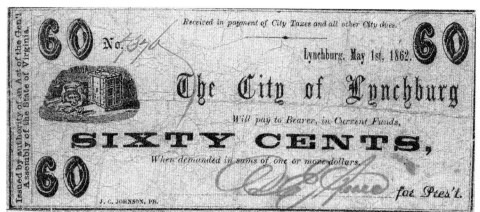

A 60¢ Confederate note issued by the City of Lynchburg in 1862. (Nathan Formo.)

HILL CITY SEMINARY,
LYNCHBURG, VIRGINIA.

The following Report exhibits the Literary standing and Deportment of *Miss Fannie Diuguid* for the week ending *May 22nd* 1868.

STUDIES.	Monday.	Tuesday.	Wednesday.	Thursday.	Friday.	REMARKS.
Roll Call	⁄	⁄	⁄	⁄	⁄	
Spelling						
Spelling with definition						
Reading	5		5		5	
Writing	5	5	5	5	5	
History						
Geography						
Dictation Exercise						
English Grammar				5		
English Composition	5					
Intellectual Arithmetic						
Written Arithmetic						
Algebra	5	5	4	5	3	
Geometry						
Trigonometry						
Mensuration						
Philology						
Latin	4	5	5	5	5	
Latin Composition						
Rhetoric		5		5		
Mental and Moral Philosophy	5		5		5	
French		6		6		
Chemistry						
Natural Philosophy						
Deportment	5	5	5	5	4	

EXPLANATIONS:—A perfect lesson is valued at 5, and its value decreases as it departs from perfection. Unexceptionable Conduct is marked 5, which is diminished as the conduct becomes objectionable.

J. E. CHRISTIAN, A. M., Principal.

The 1868 report card of Fannie Diuguid, a student at the Hill City Seminary. (Collection of Dorothy Potter.)

Lynch's Mill on Blackwater Creek, 1870. (Jones Memorial Library.)

Abram Biggers, Lynchburg's first superintendent of schools, 1870. (Jones Memorial Library.)

Freedmen's School, 1870. (Sesquicentennial Committee.)

A view of Church Street footbridge from 12th Street in 1870. (Jones Memorial Library.)

The Winfree Home at 10th and Wise Streets was once part of the original Lynchburg College. (Jones Memorial Library.)

The office of the Lynchburg News, *1880. (Jones Memorial Library.)*

Would-be soldiers at play, 1880. (Mrs. John James.)

One of the last horse-drawn trolley cars in Lynchburg, 1887. (The Lynchburg News.*)*

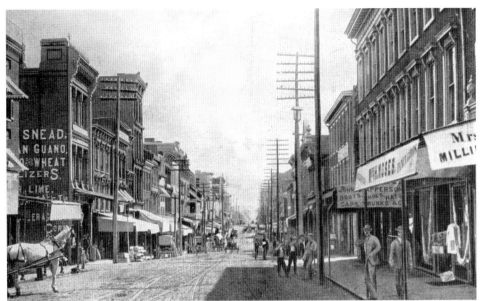

Main Street in 1880. (Jones Memorial Library.)

The 5th Street Fire Station, 1890. (Jones Memorial Library.)

A pint-sized citizen exercises a giant-sized dog, 1890. (Jones Memorial Library.)

The second grade at Biggers Elementary School, 1891. (W.R.C. Dameron.)

Lynchburg troops leaving for the Spanish-American War in 1898. (Jones Memorial Library.)

*The board of
the Friends
Tobacco
Warehouse,
1890. (Jones
Memorial
Library.)*

*Buffalo Bill's pre-show parade including German-style cavalry, or uhlans, comes
to town in 1899. (Jones Memorial Library.)*

An entry in the Lynchburg Flower Parade on Court Street, 1900. (Jones Memorial Library.)

The ruins of the South River Meetinghouse, 1900. (Jones Memorial Library.)

Main Street in 1900. (Jones Memorial Library.)

A backyard swing in Lynchburg, 1900. (Jones Memorial Library.)

Men of the Lynchburg Gun Club take a rest after a summer morning's sport, 1900. (Jones Memorial Library.)

Tobacco workers take a break in 1898. (Jones Memorial Library.)

*Senator John Warwick Daniel, "The
Lame Lion of Virginia," 1900.
(Jones Memorial Library.)*

*Bust of Gregory Willis Hayes, President
of Virginia Seminary and College,
1891–1906. (Dorothy Potter)*

A fashionable parlor at the end of the nineteenth century. (Jones Memorial Library.)

C.M. Guggenheimer Department Store advertisement, 1903. (The Lynchburg News.)

Almond Dry Goods advertisement from 1903 (The Lynchburg News).

Rivermont Park Casino, 1905. (Jones Memorial Library.)

*The Academy of
Music fire, 1911.
(Jones Memorial
Library.)*

*The faculty and the senior class on graduation day at Virginia Christian College
in 1907. (Lynchburg College.)*

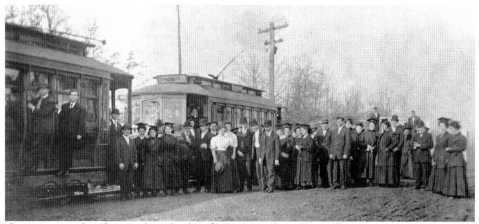

Streetcars take the student body of Virginia Christian College to Church in 1908. (Lynchburg College.)

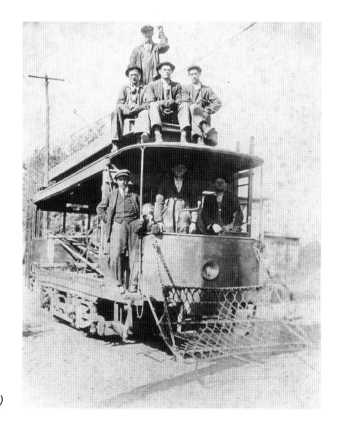

Maintenance crew on a Lynchburg trolley, 1910. (Jones Memorial Library.)

Students on the front lawn of Virginia Christian College, Westover Hall in the background, 1906. (Lynchburg College.)

Boy Scouts take a break while hiking in 1915. (The Lynchburg News.)

Local troops leaving Lynchburg in the summer of 1917. (Jones Memorial Library.)

The ladies of the Lynchburg Chapter of the American Red Cross at their railway station canteen, 1918. (Jones Memorial Library.)

A parade down Main Street marking the end of World War I, 1919. (The Lynchburg News.)

HOME

OF THE

PIEDMONT MOTOR CAR CO., Inc.

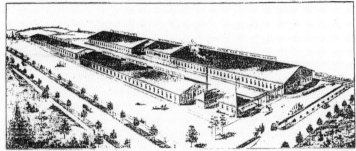

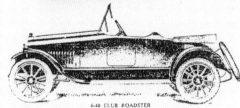

6-40 CLUB ROADSTER

The present home of the Piedmont Motor Car Co., Inc., *and its product*, developed from an idea to a modern equipped plant with capacity of 2000 finished motor cars per annum. In January, 1917, the company moved into the first unit of its plant, and in March of that year turned out its first finished cars. Since then six additional units have been completed, giving an aggregate of 40,000 sq. ft. floor space. The last addition being one of the most modernly equipped body making plants in the country, with a capacity of 30 completed bodies a day.

For 1918 the Company announces several new styles, consisting of Roadsters and Touring cars in both four and six cylinder models. These are of the latest design and in appearance and workmanship are surpassed by none.

No longer a stranger but a tried and tested friend with *Style*, *Comfort*, and above all *Durability*, built in every Piedmont.

Values offered in the cars shown here may seem too good to be true, but they are true and are made possible by close attention to every mechanical detail, careful buying and standardized production.

The enthusiastic welcome given the now popular 1917 Piedmont-30, is being repeated, and large orders are being booked daily.

The demand for the company's product is far in excess of the present production facilities and an increased capacity is being planned.

The Piedmont-30 five-passenger, announced a year ago was the sensation of the season and became instantly popular in the ten different states in which the entire first year's production was distributed.

4-30 TOURING

For Particulars, detailed specification price and terms on open territory, address

Piedmont Motor Car Co., Inc.

Lexington Turnpike and Southern Railway
LYNCHBURG, VA.

6-40 SPEEDSTER TOURING

An advertisement for The Piedmont Motor Car Company, 1918. (The Lynchburg News.)

Rivermont Bridge, c. 1906. (Jones Memorial Library.)

An aerial view of Sweet Briar College in 1924. (Jones Memorial Library.)

Monument Terrace with the dolphin fountain, 1925. (Jones Memorial Library.)

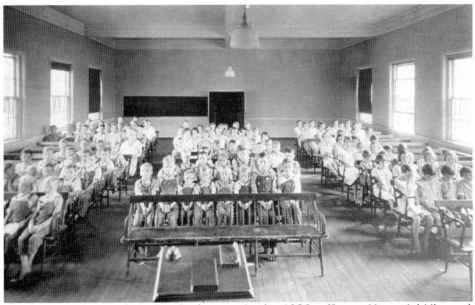

Students at the Presbyterian Orphanage in the 1920s. (Jones Memorial Library.)

A Lynchburg public school classroom, 1925. (Jones Memorial Library.)

The Clay Street Reservoir, Lynchburg's main water supply in the 1920s and 1930s. (Jones Memorial Library.)

Poetess Anne Spencer photographed around 1925 in front of Dunbar High School where she served as librarian. (Carol Spencer Read.)

The dedication of Charles Keck's "The Listening Post," November 11, 1926. (The Lynchburg News.)

An Arbor Day observance from the early 1930s. (Jones Memorial Library.)

The final reunion of the veterans of the Garland-Rodes Camp of Confederate Veterans in 1934. (Jones Memorial Library.)

The Lynchburg Sesquicentennial Half Dollar, with Senator Carter Glass on the obverse, 1936. (Nathan Formo.)

Main Street in 1936. (Jones Memorial Library.)

Chauncey Spencer, the son of poetess Anne Spencer, was a pioneer black aviator who paved the way for the famous Tuskeegee Airmen. This photograph was taken in 1937. (Carol Spencer Read.)

Virginia Polytechnic Institute's Marching Band on Main Street, November 1941. (Jones Memorial Library.)

Reverend I.W. Harper and church leaders, St. James C.M.E. Church, 1945. (Steva Burton.)

City League basketball team, 1948. (Jones Memorial Library.)

Train arriving at the Southern (Kemper Street) Station in the 1960s. (The Lynchburg News.)

Waiting to take the field in 1950. (Jones Memorial Library.)

A surprise birthday party for James Garrison, "Mr. Jim," the chief baker at Lynchburg College, 1957. (Lynchburg College.)

The Lynchburg College men's soccer team and coaches Bill Shellenberger and Dale Almond celebrate winning the Mason-Dixon Conference title, 1959. (Lynchburg College.)

*Hundley Hall Beatles,
Lynchburg College, 1964.
(Dorothy Potter)*

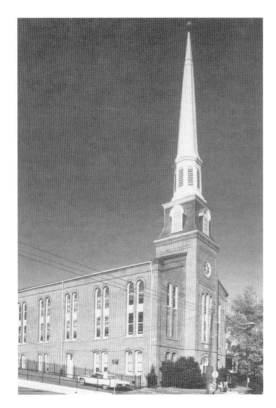

*Court Street Baptist Church,
the home of one of the oldest
African-American congregations
in Lynchburg. (Jones Memorial
Library.)*

School days, 1976. (Jones Memorial Library)

"The Mayor's Medal" for Lynchburg's Bicentennial, by Edmund D. Potter. Struck in aluminum, it was a free souvenir for the 1986 celebration. (Edmund Potter)

The Hillside Garden Club enjoys a luncheon meeting at the Station House Museum in the Old City Cemetery, 2002. (Southern Memorial Association.)

The batteau Fluvanna *before the race to Richmond, 2003. (Dorothy Potter.)*

Chapter Six

"WHAT MIGHT HAVE BEEN"

1865–1886

Bruce Catton's 1953 prize-winning best seller was entitled *A Stillness at Appomattox*. Paralysis is perhaps the best word to describe Lynchburg in that fateful month of April 1865. Thanks to the efforts of General Early, the city had been spared the physical destruction that left Richmond in ruins, but the Hill City's economy was in a shambles. In 1863, the Confederate government ordered all farmers to devote their efforts to growing edible crops, and by the time of the surrender the fields were already plowed and planted with foodstuffs. Thus the tobacco factories would not reach their normal production capacity for over a year. The warehouses were empty, save for evidence that they had recently been used to shelter the wounded and dying; the black tobacco factory workers had been assigned to war duties in 1863, and many vanished into the general population after emancipation.

During the months that followed plugs of tobacco became more valuable than bullion, but by 1865 even this form of "money" was depleted. Many of the stores were vacant, their goods having disappeared months, even years earlier. Veterans in patched or tattered uniforms mingled with freed slaves from the surrounding counties, shuffling up and down the dusty streets looking for work, or seeking a bit of early spring sunshine in the deserted doorway of a dilapidated building. It seemed that the only people regularly employed in earning a livelihood in Lynchburg were the women of the Buzzard, and the saloon keepers.

The Union occupation under General Mackensie was brief, and for a while Lynchburg was without a garrison. Then General J. Irvin Gregg was assigned to the city, assisted by Lieutenant-Colonel Duncan as the Provost-Marshal. They were charged with administering the oath of allegiance to the United States to all adult males who had served the Confederate States in any capacity. The city's newspapers resumed publication in May 1865, and their carefully censored editions were used to disseminate federal directives, particularly the necessity of taking the oath as soon as possible.

When Andrew Johnson, the only Southern senator who remained in Congress when his state seceded from the Union, became president after Lincoln's assassination, he disclosed his intention to follow a reconstruction policy similar to that conceived by his predecessor. With the exception of Confederate civil and military officers and the very wealthy—whom he personally despised—most Southerners who took the oath of allegiance would receive a pardon and amnesty. They would not be compensated for the loss of their slaves, but they would be eligible to be elected as delegates to state conventions. This would restore a legitimate government by rejecting secession, repudiating state debts incurred between 1861 and 1865, and ratifying the Thirteenth Amendment that abolished slavery. Hoping to gain extra votes in 1868, Johnson granted thousands of pardons to ex-Confederates who should have been disenfranchised. It was an ill-conceived strategy that would jeopardize his presidency and in time force the former states of the Confederacy to endure a far more severe form of reconstruction.

The first federal officers assigned to Lynchburg fully supported law and order, and thus they enjoyed a compatible relationship with the city's civilian leaders during the early months of presidential reconstruction. Gregg ordered his Provost-Marshall to confiscate the local supply of liquor, and then he closed the bars. The prostitutes were arrested and detained in a tobacco warehouse, which was converted into a workhouse. This proved but a temporary solution to an old problem.

While the business climate appeared dismal in what had once been the second wealthiest city in the United States, Lynchburg was actually on the verge of a modest economic recovery. Although the Confederate currency was worthless, a number of citizens, like the proverbial prudent Frenchman, began to utilize the bullion they had quietly hidden in 1861. The pre-war banks had vanished, but on August 11, 1865, First National Bank was organized. Twelve days later Lynchburg National Bank was founded. Both institutions made use of the resources of those residents who had not put their full faith in "the Cause," but in United States gold. Their financial acumen quickly attracted Northern investors.

If the situation of the poorer whites appeared hopeless, that of the blacks was desperate. Only the existence of the Freedmens' Bureau on Main Street prevented mass starvation. There was a brief attempt to revive an idea that had enjoyed limited success in Virginia a generation earlier; under the auspices of the Lynchburg Emigration Society, 150 local African Americans left for a new life in Liberia on October 31, 1865. For those who remained, education was perceived as the path to new opportunities. While there were separate private schools for white boys and girls whose parents could afford the tuition, the conservative elite saw educated blacks and poorer whites as a threat to social order. Jacob Yoder, the superintendent of the Freedmens' schools, and the men, women, and children who were his students were subjected to constant intimidation.

"What Might Have Been": 1865–1886

The news from Washington did not bode well for those who sought to regain the power and control they had enjoyed before the war. The struggle between the President and the Radical Republicans in Congress was approaching a climax. A packed public meeting held in Lynchburg on February 22, 1866, endorsed the policies of President Johnson, but it was only a symbolic display. 1866 proved a year of gestures. On May 10, the anniversary of the death of General Stonewall Jackson, the first Confederate Memorial Day was observed in Lynchburg. While the Southern states had been forced to ratify the Thirteenth Amendment, this action initially proved to be only an empty formality. Real equality remained elusive because they instituted "black codes" that created a landless, dependent black labor force with legal freedom and little else. The Freedmens' Bureau and the Union army retarded the total enforcement of the codes with limited success.

When the Thirty-ninth Congress met in December 1865, the Radical Republicans began the process of dismantling the black codes and denying former Confederates their civil rights. Johnson refused to make any concessions, and his stubbornness drove the Moderate Republicans into an alliance with the Radicals. First, Congress voted to continue the Freedmen's Bureau for three years, giving it the power to run special military courts. Johnson vetoed the measure in February 1866. The following month, Congress passed a bill that made African Americans full citizens, and Johnson vetoed this civil rights bill. This measure became the first major law ever passed over a presidential veto. In April, Congress passed the Fourteenth Amendment, the first federal effort to restrict state control of civil and political rights. Only Tennessee approved it, and thereby avoided further reconstruction.

In July the Supplementary Freedmen's Bureau Act was revived and passed over Johnson's veto, but the Fourteenth Amendment was the main issue of the congressional election of 1866. It proved a Republican triumph. The debate over the fate of the South began in December 1866, and it ended with the Reconstruction Act of 1867. The Confederate States, excluding Tennessee, were divided into five military districts, each under a Union general. Once each state ratified the Fourteenth Amendment, and it had become part of the Federal Constitution, the state would be re-admitted and reconstruction would be ended.

On January 20, 1867, Lynchburg was buried by a snow storm. Congressional Reconstruction began on March 5 and the city was then buried under federal regulations. A week later, General Schofield was put in charge of Military District One—Virginia—and General Wilcox was assigned to Lynchburg. Union soldiers stationed in the city soon found their way to the houses and bars along Jefferson Street. While the money they spent on their leisure activities was a welcomed addition to the local economy, their brawls and drunkenness threatened military discipline and public order. With his patience at an end, in the summer of 1867, Colonel George P. Buell issued General Order Number 61, which again closed the bordellos at Buzzard Roost, Tin Shingles, and Curl's Row. However, even pushing one of the shanties into the river with the residents still inside only briefly deterred the continuation of disreputable business activities on the banks of the James River.

Perhaps the most positive result of Reconstruction in Lynchburg was the creation of a public education system, which in time became the city's pride. When General N.M. Curtis was in charge of Lynchburg, he sought the support of the clergy in the formation of a public school system financed with fines. He proposed four schools for white students and two schools for black students. Finally, on January 24, 1870, Virginia was readmitted to the Union, and the following October there were a series of open discussions on public education. On April 5, 1871, the first free public schools were opened in Lynchburg. They were nine in number, and children were separated by sex, religion, and race. The following February, the first high school opened.

In 1877 the city council decided to close the high school, citing rising costs. The more reactionary members were probably also concerned that poorer children might assume an education would entitle them to a position of equality with their betters. This was an attitude not confined to Lynchburg, Virginia, or the South. At the end of the nineteenth century, free secondary education was considered by many as a potential threat to the established social order. Abram Biggers, the first Superintendent of the Lynchburg School System, fought for the re-opening of the high school and he had the majority of the electorate behind him.

Fearful of losing their seats in the next election, the members of council bowed to the will of the people and re-opened the high school in the fall of 1879. Biggers did not live to savor this victory. His tireless efforts on behalf of secondary education hastened his death from tuberculosis on March 28, 1879. He had served Lynchburg as superintendent from 1870 until 1878; his successor, Edward Christian Glass, would serve until 1931.

The average Lynchburg citizen was less concerned with supposed threats to the national social order than the everyday events of life in the City of Seven Hills. The first edition of the *Lynchburg News* appeared on January 15, 1866, and a month later it announced that the discovery of oil in Central Virginia would cure the city's economic ills. The Campbell County Oil Company was quickly organized and those with money rushed to buy stock. Oil was selling at $1 per gallon on the national market, an unheard-of sum at the time. The equipment soon arrived and drilling began. This led to the creation of the Lynchburg Mining and Petroleum Company. After drilling down to 600 feet without finding anything, the "developers" quietly left town with all their assets. Lynchburg's one and only oil boom was done.

Far more promising were the new industries founded in Lynchburg before 1886. Finally the city's economy was achieving the diversity that would allow it to weather the economic storms of the late nineteenth and early twentieth centuries. Steel, machine-made furniture, shoes, nails, vehicles, and leather goods would in time replace tobacco as the foundation of the city's economy. However, since these were skilled trades, this long anticipated diversity did not immediately mean improved conditions for poor white laborers. Many of them were forced by necessity to take jobs they would never have considered before the war—employment in the tobacco factories formerly reserved for slaves.

Out of desperation and necessity evolved a common cause that briefly transcended racial barriers, and momentarily in the 1880s the Lynchburg laboring class dominated the political life of the city. Despite the existence of the Klu Klux Klan in Lynchburg, African-American men like Jefferson Anderson and Henry Edwards were freely elected to the city council from a predominately black ward, anticipating by 80 years the true democratization of the city's government. For the post–Civil War white generation it was the realization of their worst nightmare. Poor whites had been dismissed with contempt for years; now wealthy power brokers began to seriously court them. As the literacy rate in this segment of the population began to rise with the advent of free public schools, their threat to the status quo became even more dangerous. In the end an appeal to an almost innate racism among poor whites, and an invention preserved the power of Lynchburg's establishment.

Before the Civil War, the proportion of free blacks in the population of Lynchburg was much higher than in other Virginia cities. With the end of the war, an independent black community began to evolve; it was centered in the newly-founded black churches and fraternal organizations led by the men and women who had always been free. They already understood the value of education, and the necessity of mastering a trade other than that of performing the menial tasks associated with the tobacco production. Slowly, under their tutelage, a generation of youngsters grew to maturity free of the stigma of slavery and ready to assume what they considered their rightful place in society despite the hostility of those poorer whites who should have been their natural allies.

Virginia inventor Jake Bonsack's realization of an efficient cigarette-rolling machine in the early 1880s transformed the tobacco consumption habits of the world, and led to the shift of major markets to Danville, Virginia and Durham, North Carolina.

Many considered this change a positive development because the post-war tobacco industry was the center of labor unrest, union organization, and more of a threat to the political establishment than the rage of those voters who wanted to save the high school. Many of the blacks who had led strikes and striven to achieve equality through the political process left Lynchburg seeking jobs in the rapidly changing tobacco industry. By the end of the century, the "right people" were once again in control of Lynchburg, and the white laborers reduced to political impotence.

With Virginia's return to the Union in 1870, national politics assumed the importance in Lynchburg that it had enjoyed before the war. Most voters considered themselves to be members of the Democratic Party, although there were certainly supporters of the Republican Party among former Unionists, transplanted Northerners, and the newly enfranchised African Americans. The election of 1876, like that of 2000, was disputed, and it was not until March 2, 1877, that Rutherford B. Hayes was declared the winner over Samuel J. Tilden when the electoral votes from Florida were assigned to the Republican electors. Despite the frustration of citizens at the outcome, when President Hayes visited the city on September 24, 1877, he was given an enthusiastic welcome as well as a gala reception and banquet. It was a much warmer greeting than the one he had received when he "visited" Sandusky in the summer of 1864 as one of General Hunter's officers. Two years later when Lynchburg author Marion Cabell Tyree's best-selling *Housekeeping in Old Virginia* appeared, it carried an endorsement from First Lady Lucy Hayes. Having tasted Lynchburg hospitality, the President now had the chance to sample Lynchburg cuisine.

Although voters supported the Democratic candidate Winfield S. Hancock in 1880, when winner President James A. Garfield died on September 19, 1881, of a wound received on July 2, the city went into mourning on July 26, the day of the slain President's funeral. On November 3, 1884, there was jubilation in Lynchburg when Grover Cleveland, a Democrat, was chosen President. In the same contest John Warwick Daniel was elected to the House of Representatives. A year later this favorite son of Lynchburg, who would soon earn the nickname of the "Lame Lion of Virginia," was elected to the Senate.

Looking back on the 21 years between the end of the Civil War and the centennial of Lynchburg's designation as a town, most people would not remember the city's brief rejection of political oligarchy, but rather the achievements and tragedies that marked those years. In May 1868, General Robert E. Lee, then President of Washington College in Lexington, had attended a Protestant Episcopal Council meeting in Lynchburg. Mothers brought their infants and small children to see the man who seemed to represent everything noble and enduring about Virginia. Two years later, on October 12, they mourned his premature death at the age of 61. On March 18, 1869, former President Andrew Johnson, the man who might have granted Lee a full pardon, was the city's guest at a public banquet. During his last visit to Lynchburg in 1861, a local mob had tried to assault him and he had held them off at gunpoint. Nine days after Johnson's departure, the eccentric local millionaire Samuel Miller died; his legacy to the city would be the park that bears his name, the city reservoir, and the orphanage that has been a haven for local girls since 1875.

A series of tragedies in the last quarter of the nineteenth century forced the city council to institute the first of numerous rigorous building codes and safety regulations that now protect the citizens of Lynchburg. On July 14, 1876, the City Hotel—formerly the Ladies Hospital, formerly the Union Hotel—collapsed from "old age." Only one adult, a guest; and one child, the daughter of the cook, were killed. Less than two years later, on May 28, 1878, another poorly-maintained building collapsed at the eastern corner of Eighth and Main Streets. At the time it had been rented to a local congregation to use for a church supper. Fortunately, when it collapsed nobody was in the building. Authorities hesitated to impose on the citizens a new set of regulations; then five months later, on October 16, 1878, tragedy struck again. There was both a wedding and a revival scheduled at the African-American Court Street Baptist Church on the same evening. Because the congregation had limited funds to spare, the building was poorly maintained. The regular service began after the wedding ceremony, but when some plaster from the ceiling fell into the main sanctuary, the congregation panicked. Ten people were killed and scores injured as terrified parishioners jumped from windows or were crushed or smothered in the melee. After the Court Street disaster, public attitudes towards codes and regulations began to slowly change.

Lynchburg owes its existence to the James River, but that stream can be a curse as well as a blessing. In September 1870, after a long dry spell, the city was drenched by the remnants of a tropical storm. In a matter of days the river was well above flood stage, and many who waited too long to leave their homes by its banks were drowned. The exact number of casualties has never been accurately determined. This "flood of the century" taught the citizenry a new fear and respect for the treacherous James. In successive torrents, the loss of life would prove minimal. In November 1877 there was another flood, and the canal was badly damaged again. Although it was repaired and re-opened from Richmond to Buchanan, its days as a viable alternative to the rail lines were numbered. Because of the damage done by the two floods, a new bridge from the city to Amherst County was a necessity. On August 14, 1878, the new toll-free iron bridge was opened. It was replaced in 1918 by the Williams Viaduct, which in turn was succeeded by the John Lynch Bridge in 1988.

LYNCHBURG

The flood of September 1870 also had a devastating effect on the slowly-recovering economy. With the coming of winter the condition of the poor became critical, but neither private nor public charity responded to their plight. Whites were unwilling to help former slaves whom they considered "ungrateful." To survive some, both black and white, turned to petty crime. The following year, the city council ordered the demolition of the old market that many considered a gathering place for criminals and stray dogs. The new city market was located on Main near 12th Street. The petty thieves were put in jail, and to solve the canine problem the city council required dog owners to purchase tags. Those without tags were shot by the police despite a public protest. Cows, however, roamed free until 1893.

As Lynchburg approached her centennial celebration, the sacrifice of the fire company was gratefully remembered. The volunteer company was reorganized at the end of the war, but by 1880 it was evident that Lynchburg needed a professional fire-fighting service. On May 30, 1883, shortly after it was organized, the Lynchburg Fire Department lost five of its members battling a blaze that threatened much of downtown. Following this tragedy, a memorial fountain portraying a fireman with a hose was erected at the foot of Courthouse Hill. Moved to Miller Park in 1922, it was destroyed in 1956 when Hurricane Hazel hit the city. It was replaced in 1976 by a granite copy through the generosity of the Altrusa Club. In the summer of 1883, while people were still mourning the loss of the five firemen, an arsonist created a panic throughout the city. He was eventually caught, but it was months before Lynchburg returned to normal.

With the return of prosperity, Lynchburg began to add the trappings of a modern urban center. On February 6, 1879, the new Opera House—the late nineteenth century equivalent of a civic center—opened on Main near the corner of Twelfth Street. Only three years after Alexander Graham Bell unveiled his 1876 invention, there was serious talk of starting a phone exchange. On October 19, 1880, the first six horse-drawn cars of Lynchburg's street railway were in use. A ride cost 10¢, or the price of a spool of thread. The first train over the Richmond and Allegheny Railroad arrived in Lynchburg on August 17, 1881. In 1882, all the buildings in the city were renumbered in preparation for free mail delivery by the Federal Postal Service. As Lynchburg prepared to celebrate its past, its future had already been altered by events its leaders could not foresee. Forces were at work in post–Civil War America that were subject to neither local nor state control.

In the immediate post-war period, the economy of the United States grew at an almost dizzying pace. The industrial revolution affected every area of production, but the field where expansion was most noticeable was transportation—especially railroads. In 1866, the citizens of Lynchburg pledged $60,000 to the building of the Lynchburg and Danville Railroad, which would in time become part of the Southern Railway. It was to be the first step in recapturing the city's place as the western hub of Virginia's railways, but the nature of the nation's transit system was undergoing a transformation.

In May of 1869, at Promontory Point in Utah, the Union Pacific and the Central Pacific were joined to form the first transcontinental railroad. The future lay in interconnected rail systems that linked the east and west coasts and those points between them. When General William Mahone replaced William L. Owen as President of the Virginia and Tennessee Railroad in 1867, he immediately attempted to initiate a union between the V&T and the Southside Railway. His plan had been rumored before his election; now it proved to be the first step in a consolidation with the Norfolk and Petersburg Railroad. Mahone was a man of vision, but his experience had taught him to command, not persuade. Led by Bishop John Early, the stockholders fought Mahone every step of the way, but they ultimately failed to stop the merger. Lynchburg was not to be the hub of the new system. An attempt was made the following year to unseat Mahone, but it failed. The new line, the Atlantic, Mississippi, and Ohio Railroad was poised by 1870 to join the 400 rail lines in the northeast and become part of the expanding transcontinental system.

Railroads consumed coal and steel at an extraordinary rate, and this stimulated further growth in these industries, making them extremely attractive to speculators. The directors of the Northern Pacific Railroad were enticed into expanding beyond their capacity to meet their obligations. This failure led to the closure of the bank that held their assets, and that started a panic that led to the collapse of the stock market, a five year depression, and eighteen thousand business failures including the Atlantic, Mississippi, and Ohio Railroad (AM&O). General Mahone's grand gamble was a casualty of the Panic of 1873.

The business leaders of Lynchburg asserted themselves when the AM&O was placed in receivership in 1876. Mahone was accused of mismanagement by men who had once been his friends and business partners. While Lynchburg's community leaders debated how to reclaim their beloved railroad, a group of investors from Philadelphia purchased the AM&O in May 1879. They then turned their attention to the Shenandoah Valley Railroad, which had been slowly moving southward. They purchased it and merged with the AM&O to create the Norfolk and Western Railway (N&W), Virginia's link to the transcontinental system. There has been much speculation and a great deal has been written about the refusal of the Lynchburg business community to permit the N&W to locate its shops in the city. To be sure, there may have been some concerns about the possibility of increased union activities and the necessity of raising wages to compete with those paid by the railway, but in truth Lynchburg was probably never seriously considered as a junction point by the Norfolk and Western.

The "new railroads" preferred to establish their terminals and junction points in very small towns where they could purchase most of the property and completely dominate future development. This was not possible in established cities like Lynchburg. The N&W would never have been able to control the city's political life or its economic destiny, but it could transform Big Lick into Roanoke, the metropolis of southwest Virginia. When the town fathers of that tiny community near Salem offered the directors of the N&W $7,500 to establish the junction of the AM&O and the Shenandoah Valley Railroad in their community, they lost control of their town for a time but in return reaped a fortune. The same astounding pattern of growth was repeated in places like Omaha, Nebraska; Oakland, California; and Tacoma, Washington, which were either junctions or terminal points of other systems. By 1911, Roanoke would replace Lynchburg as the most important urban center west of Richmond, and by 1952 Roanoke's economic supremacy led to her political dominance of western Virginia.

Chapter Seven

"WELCOME STRANGERS
TO OUR GATES"
1886–1914

Lynchburgers had given only cursory attention to America's centennial celebration in Philadelphia in 1876. Remembrances from the Civil War remained painful, and having rejoined the Union only six years earlier, some felt there was little to celebrate. However the city's centennial was another matter; Lynchburg now had an opportunity to resume her place among the leading communities in the commonwealth. Led by a small group of influential businessmen, including Senator John Warwick Daniel, philanthropist Max Guggenheimer and others, a public meeting was held in which committees were organized and various options explored.

1886 was chosen, based on the General Assembly's charter to John Lynch and his associates, rather than the opening of the ferry service, which had in fact launched the town. *The Virginian*, *The News*, and *The Advance* ran promotional stories about the city's history and plans for the event, which was set for October 12–15. On opening day, a large banner stretched across Main Street proclaiming "Welcome Strangers to Our Gates." Lynchburg's gates were non-existent, but the "strangers" arrived in force; according to various accounts, including a centennial booklet, visitors numbered around 25,000, more than double the city's population.

Such demonstrations of civil pride were frequent in late nineteenth-century America. Like other communities South and North, Lynchburg celebrated both history and modernity—notably its hardware and tobacco firms. Having survived floods, fires, war, economic trials, and Reconstruction, its tradesmen's parade, decorated buildings, agricultural show, fireworks, poetry, speeches, and music were elements of a healing process. The planting of a Centennial Oak at the Fairgrounds on November 29 was yet more proof that Lynchburg was ready to embrace the future.

This sense of optimism was evident in another late nineteenth-century phenomenon: a land boom. As early as 1882, a Chamber of Commerce had been organized to encourage businesses to locate in the Hill City. A plethora of land companies appeared, including the James River, Park Avenue, Rivermont, East Lynchburg, West Lynchburg, and Lynchburg Land and Improvement Company.

Wealthy citizens like Senator Daniel, a major investor in the Lynchburg & Durham Railroad and president of the West Lynchburg Land Company, predicted great things, and Lynchburg seemed poised to respond. In 1888, Richmond had become the first American city to successfully introduce electric streetcars; Lynchburg converted its horse-drawn cars to electric ones in 1891. Lines ran from Main Street to the West Lynchburg Land Company's resort hotel and, on the other side of town, to Rivermont Park, part of the development of the Rivermont Land Company. Brick sidewalks were laid, and by 1893 an ordinance prevented cows from grazing freely within the city limits. Some visionaries dreamed of a new Pittsburgh by the James. Though this proved ephemeral, the Rivermont and West Lynchburg Land Companies facilitated legacies more valuable than mere lots, bricks, and mortar.

In her August 1890 essay "Good Times for Old Virginia," local author and feminist Orra Gray Langhorne described the flurry of activity among the land companies:

> We have found much amusement in seeing the numerous real
> estate agents, mostly young men, intensely busy, rushing
> about, putting up signboards with the names of their firms,
> attending sales, and riding up and down the road behind a
> pair of dashing steeds. Sometimes these very energetic
> persons vary the monotony of business by taking young
> ladies with them on their drives. . . .

The "boomers," as Mrs. Langhorne called them, worked hard to promote the area, but amid glowing descriptions of Lynchburg's climate, scenic beauty, railways, religious establishments, and manufacturing opportunities, one element—higher education—was missing. Old Lynchburg College was fast becoming a memory; the nearest colleges were in Salem, Lexington, or Charlottesville. Senator Daniel had noted this in his centennial speech, exhorting Lynchburgers to:

> Spread wide your city limits. . . . fight "old fogyism" and "pull-
> backism" wherever you find them. . . . Establish here a female
> college of the highest grade . . . Wake up, Lynchburg!

Considering the conservatism of the community, elements of which had recently opposed a public high school, it is remarkable that within less than 20 years of Daniel's call to action Lynchburg became home to three educational movements radical for their time: higher education for African-Americans, academically rigorous college education for women, and a co-educational college. These forces of change grew from three denominations: the Baptists, Methodists, and the Disciples of Christ.

"Welcome Strangers to Our Gates": 1886–1914

In May 1887, the Virginia State Baptist Convention, which included both white and black members, chose Lynchburg as the site for its African-American college, Virginia Seminary and Normal School. Incorporated by the General Assembly on February 24, 1888, the Seminary—later renamed Virginia College, and currently the Virginia University of Lynchburg—was also supported by other African-American churches and a core of black businessmen. Like many schools of the era, it included a program for students to complete their secondary education, a vital component since Virginia had so long lacked public schools, and education for African Americans was still largely confined to technical skills.

Virginia Seminary's second president Gregory Willis Hayes, who served from 1891 to 1906, strongly believed in autonomy for black educational institutions. He and his supporters were often at odds with the State Baptist Convention and some of the seminary's trustees, who wanted financial support from white organizations like the American Baptist Home Mission Society, even if that meant accepting their guidelines on what subjects should be taught.

American Baptists, a northern branch of Baptists who had split with their southern counterparts over slavery in 1840, had been abolitionists and traditional advocates of black education. However, in the 1880s they chose to support schools that offered primarily industrial and technical courses. President Hayes, a graduate of Oberlin College with a degree in mathematics, insisted that liberal arts remain a vital part of the seminary's curriculum.

Gregory Hayes served two terms as the seminary's president. A marble bust at the college describes him as an "Educator, Orator, Race Leader." After his death in 1906, his wife Mary Rice Hayes, who also taught at the school, became at age 30 its interim president for two years. Born in 1875 in Harrisonburg, Virginia, to Confederate General John R. Jones and his African-American servant Malinda Rice, Mary was acknowledged and educated by her white father. As much a pioneer for civil rights as her late husband, Mary Rice Hayes was a founder of Lynchburg's first NAACP chapter in 1913. After her second marriage to Danville lawyer William Allen, she moved to Montclair, New Jersey, and became a leader in the integration movement in that city.

Anne Scales Spencer, a close friend of Mary Hayes Allen, would become Virginia Seminary's most famous graduate. Born in Henry County, Virginia, in 1882, Anne Bannister Scales spent much of her early life in West Virginia. In 1893 she came to Virginia Seminary, the youngest student then enrolled. Overcoming that difficulty as well as a lack of previous formal education (she taught herself to read at age eight) she graduated from the seminary in 1899 as valedictorian of her class. She met Edward Spencer at the seminary, and they were married in 1901.

Fostering his wife's unique gifts, Edward hired housekeepers so Anne could devote herself to writing and creating the elaborate garden that she described as "half my world." He also built her a cottage she named "Edankraal," where she went to more privately read and work. For more than two decades, beginning in 1924, she served as librarian for the all-black Dunbar High School.

Following World War I, Anne and Edward Spencer entertained many notable African-American leaders who came through Lynchburg, including George Washington Carver, W.E.B. Dubois, James Weldon Johnson, Paul Robeson, Marian Anderson, Langston Hughes, Thurgood Marshall, Mary McLeod Bethune, and Dr. Martin Luther King Jr. James Weldon Johnson encouraged her writing and composed part of his poem "The Creation" at the Spencers. However, in a world dominated by "Jim Crow" laws, which she actively opposed, Anne Spencer remained relatively unknown in Lynchburg until the 1970s.

Among Virginia Seminary's early supporters was Adolphus Humbles. Born free in 1848, Humbles first worked in a tobacco factory and later on a packet boat. Becoming a stockman and owner of a general store, he soon expanded his interests to a livery stable and a grading and paving company. These businesses enabled Humbles to contribute generously to Virginia Seminary; he paid the mortgage held by the Baptist Home Mission Society, and as treasurer of the Seminary helped finance the construction of several buildings. One of these, Humbles Hall, was named in his honor. His death in 1926 would deprive the school of a dedicated friend.

If Gregory Hayes had lived he and his wife, like the Spencers, would have found themselves increasingly at odds with the racist views of Carter Glass. The youngest son of a newspaper publisher, Glass, like Benjamin Franklin, began work as a "printer's devil" while in his teens. Moving from reporter to editor of *The News*, he purchased it in 1888. In 1891 Glass bought the 69-year-old *Virginian*, the second oldest daily in the state. Merging the two, he acquired Lynchburg's last paper, *The Daily Advance*, two years later. His monopoly would deprive the city of diverse media opinions for generations, and facilitated his political ambitions. Glass became a state senator in 1899.

Like many southern whites whose youth had been shaped by the Civil War and Reconstruction, Glass was a thorough Democrat who gave short shrift to any other political affiliations—Independent, Republican, or Socialist. Nor was he receptive to the aspirations of African Americans, the concerns of working-class whites, or the women's suffrage movement, which was gaining momentum in the Western states if not the South.

In 1902 Glass, Daniel, and other conservative politicians rewrote Virginia's constitution, including in it the institution of a $1.50 poll tax and a literacy test; both limited participation by blacks and poorer whites in government. That same year Glass was elected to the House of Representatives. Assigned a place on the Banking and Currency Committee, he spent a decade becoming knowledgeable in this field. His expertise changed American monetary practices in 1913 with his successful proposal to create the Federal Reserve System.

Like John Warwick Daniel, George Morgan Jones was interested in a local college for women. A bank president and partner with his brothers-in-law in Jones & Watts, the largest hardware company outside of Richmond with branches in Bedford, Danville, and Roanoke, Jones was influential in the Rivermont Company, which had land available for such an endeavor. According to early Lynchburg historian C. Asbury Christian, Jones encountered Dr. William Waugh Smith, president of Randolph-Macon College for men in Ashland, Virginia, on a streetcar and urged him to establish a women's college in Lynchburg. More than 100 fellow citizens contributed their support, and by March 1891 an agreement was reached between the Rivermont Company and Randolph-Macon's trustees. The company offered 20 acres, stock, and an endowment of $100,000. Randolph-Macon provided seed money and the College's first president, Dr. Smith.

The April opening of a massive bridge connecting downtown to the new Rivermont suburb solved a major transportation problem for Randolph-Macon. Noisily celebrated with train whistles and cannon fire, and later a banquet for the city's civic leaders at the Opera House, Rivermont Bridge was a marvel of engineering for its day. Built of iron and 136 feet high—only three feet lower than the Brooklyn Bridge—its 1,200-foot length spanned the gorge cut by Blackwater Creek at the northern end of Main Street. Its $111,000 cost showed how seriously Lynchburg entrepreneurs were prepared to support urban growth. The Rivermont development in time stretched about five miles and included elegant homes, Randolph-Macon, new churches and schools, a public park, and shopping areas. It became, in fact, one of the first planned suburbs in the nation.

Randolph-Macon began its initial session with 77 students and 12 teachers on September 14, 1893. In its early years it was still very much out in the country, since most of the Rivermont Company's acreage lay in Campbell County. The college did not become part of the city until a 1908 annexation. Geographically, Randolph-Macon's students and teachers lived at the end of the streetcar line, and some stories in *The News* and *The Daily Advance* about events near "the Woman's College" gave the impression that the young women were living a wilderness experience. Randolph-Macon opened amid a nationwide depression; even a decade later an article in the 1903 yearbook *The Helianthus* asked for more books to fill the library George M. Jones had endowed in memory of his daughters Georgie and Lillie, who had died in their teens in 1884 and 1885.

Possibly the most notable of all the graduates of Randolph-Macon Woman's College was Pearl Sydenstricker Buck (class of 1914). In 1932 she was awarded a Pulitzer Prize for her novel *The Good Earth*, and in 1938 she became the first American woman to receive the Nobel Prize for Literature. In her honor Randolph-Macon Woman's College inaugurated the Pearl S. Buck Award to recognize women for their accomplishments in the realm of world affairs. Among the recipients are former Philippines President Corazon Aquino, Bangladesh Prime Minister Shiekh Hasina, Jenan Sedat, peace activist and widow of Anwar Sedat, and Irish President Mary Robinson.

An unusually cold spring in 1893 heralded an economic chill that led to a nationwide depression lasting several years. Banks failed and there were strikes and urban riots. Only one Lynchburg bank closed in 1897, but the land boom was finished. Several companies went bankrupt, most notably the West Lynchburg Land Company, whose ambitious program had included the construction of a large summer-resort hotel. Designed by the noted New York firm of Rose and Stone, it was built in the fashionable chateau style and modeled on the French Renaissance palace, Chambord. Like many luxury hotels of the era, Westover was situated near mineral springs; guests who wished to "take the waters" could ride the streetcar and stay in the hotel or one of several nearby cottages. The resort complex opened with fanfare on July 4, 1891, but by 1896 the West Lynchburg Land Company was in receivership.

Amid the depression a political crisis in Cuba provided a distraction and increased national interest in America's role as a world power. Spain's attempts to suppress a rebellion in its Cuban colony attracted widespread sympathy for the rebels. Anti-Spanish feelings intensified with accounts of overcrowded concentration camps and terrorization of Cuba's civilian population. Sensational stories in Joseph Pulitzer's *The World* and William Randolph Hearst's *Evening Journal* were reprinted in local papers. The excuse for war occurred on February 15, 1898, with the explosion of the United States battleship *Maine* in Havana harbor. Most Americans incorrectly assumed that this was a deliberate act by Spain's government.

The Spanish-American War, which officially began in mid-April 1898, muted sectionalism temporarily, as both Union and Confederate veterans and their families saw their sons off to fight what they perceived to be a common enemy. A Lynchburg sailor, Nicholas Smith, was one of 266 men killed on the *Maine*. Local feelings ran high, but the war's brevity limited its effects on central Virginia.

Lynchburg raised three companies in response to President McKinley's call for 200,000 volunteers, but unlike Colonel Theodore Roosevelt's "Rough Riders," they got no closer to Cuba than the Florida coast. Peace was declared on August 12, 1898, and by the next month soldiers from the Zouaves, the Home Guard, and the Fitz Lee Rifles returned home. Many of them probably reassembled on April 23, 1900, for the laying of the cornerstone of the Confederate Memorial at the top of Lynchburg Hill (later renamed Monument Terrace).

A new century found Lynchburg again evaluating its potential. A special edition of The *Lynchburg News* subtitled "Incomparable Facilities in Transportation, Trade, and Manufacturing," detailed the material and spiritual virtues of the Hill City, from dentists and tobacco companies to churches and schools. The tone was optimistic; technology, science, and spirituality would conquer the ills of former ages. New churches had been built and others remodeled; businesses and educational institutions were being established.

One of these was Sweet Briar College. Built on the estate of Indiana Fletcher Williams 12 miles from Lynchburg, it received a state charter in 1901 as a school for women. In September 1906, Sweet Briar opened with 4 buildings, 36 students, and 11 teachers. The inspiration for its founding was Mrs. Williams' only child Daisy, who like the Joneses' daughters, had died in her teens.

Perhaps the most remarkable educator associated with Sweet Briar during its first 50 years was Dr. Meta Glass, its president from 1925 to 1946. She was the younger sister of Dr. Edward Christian Glass and Senator Carter Glass. Recognized by the French government for her work during World War I, she later served as the president of the Virginia Association of Colleges and the American Association of Colleges. She earned her Ph.D. degree from Columbia University and was the recipient of eight honorary doctorates.

During Dr. Glass's administration the college was served by a number of remarkable scholars including Dr. Belle Boone Beard. A 1923 graduate of Lynchburg College, Dr. Beard taught sociology at Sweet Briar from 1931 to 1963. With advanced degrees from Bryn Mawr, she made aging her area of expertise. Even in retirement she continued to work tirelessly in the interests of older citizens. She was instrumental in establishing the first White House Conference on Aging. In 1970 Governor Linwood Holton named her the Outstanding Older Virginian. For her work in gerontology she received the International Woman's Year Citation in 1975, and a year later was awarded the Military and Hospitaller Order of Saint Lazarus of Jerusalem. The oldest of Lynchburg College's six Centers of Distinction is the Belle Boone Center on Aging and the Life Course.

Among the graduates of Sweet Briar during the tenure of Dr. Glass was Elizabeth Morton Forsyth (class of 1936). Until her death in December 2003, she devoted her public life to making her community a better place in which to live. For 60 years Elizabeth Forsyth served on the board of C.B. Fleet, the pharmaceutical firm founded by her grandfather, Charles Browne Fleet, in 1869. She endowed numerous academic honors and scholarships, as well as actively supporting the arts, but it was in the area of service to her fellow citizens that her true legacy lies. In 1992 she founded Miriam's House, a transitional refuge for homeless women and children, and five years later she established Elizabeth's Early Learning Center, a nationally recognized facility that serves the needs of children from every ethnic and socio-economic group in Lynchburg.

In 1903 the Reverend Frank F. Bullard, pastor of the First Christian Church (Disciples of Christ), advised his teacher and mentor Josephus Hopwood, a Union veteran anxious to bring higher education to the South and who had already established Milligan College in Tennessee in 1881, that an ideal site in Lynchburg was available for a coeducational institution. Bullard had in mind the 120-room Westover Hotel and the acres surrounding it. Despite attempts to promote the hotel after the demise of its parent company, it had not proved economically viable as a summer resort.

Josephus Hopwood and his wife Sarah LaRue strongly believed in coeducation, later describing it in their collective autobiography as "God's Divine Plan." However, in an age when women's public and private roles were limited by law and custom, the idea of young men and women sharing the same curriculum worried some traditionalists. The Hopwoods and supporters like Reverend Bullard, who became the first president of the new Virginia Christian College's Board of Trustees, had to reassure the public that female students were carefully protected. For example, boys and girls could not sit side-by-side in classes or at meals unless they were brother and sister.

Opening in September 1903 with 155 students, Virginia Christian College was the state's second coeducational college. Westover Hall—now a dormitory, dining facility, academic and administration building—would serve multiple needs for 67 years. A men's dormitory named for Andrew Carnegie, who had uncharacteristically donated $20,000 to a structure not a library, and an academic building inspired by the University of Virginia's Rotunda and later named Hopwood Hall, were both completed in 1909.

Virginia Christian College had just begun its first session when the Hill City learned of a local disaster, which in time inspired a popular ballad. On September 27, 1903, the Southern Railroad's mail train Number 97, in route from Washington to Atlanta and running late, crossed the steep grade over the James, raced through Lynchburg, and on to a destination it would never reach. Just north of Danville "Old 97," with its whistle screaming, jumped the tracks and plunged into a ravine, killing 11 people including the engineer and injuring half a dozen more. From this destruction came "The Wreck of the Old 97," set to the tune of a nineteenth-century folk song. First recorded in 1927 by Henry Whitter, it has long been a favorite of country singers, and gave some of central Virginia's railroad towns and cities fleeting fame:

> They gave him his orders down in Monroe, Virginia,
> Saying "Steve, you're way behind time,
> This is not 38—this is Old 97,
> You must get her to Spencer on time."

****

> It's a mighty rough road from Lynchburg to Danville,
> And a line on a three-mile grade.
> And it was on that grade that he lost his air brakes,
> You should have seen the jump he made. . . .

In 1903, a few young women in Virginia were experiencing some of the educational opportunities enjoyed by their fathers and brothers, but not until the 1920 ratification of the Nineteenth Amendment could they vote in national elections. Still, the early twentieth century saw more efforts at self-fulfillment. On November 25, 1903, 11 Lynchburg ladies began to study parliamentary law and procedure; by 1907 the Woman's Club of Lynchburg had organized the Virginia Federation of Women's Clubs, creating a network of women eager to promote cultural, civic, and educational causes, like increased opportunities for women in Virginia's public college system. This objective was partially achieved with the opening of Mary Washington College in Fredericksburg in 1948–1949.

Higher education for minorities and women, coeducational colleges, women's suffrage, electric lighting and streetcars, and horseless carriages all had older Americans surely wondering where this would end. People were even openly consuming cola beverages reputed to be dangerously addictive. In 1906, a local legislator led efforts to ban Virginia sales of Coca-Cola, which was in his words, "no drink for a Christian" in Virginia. But even he had to admit that Coca-Cola was an enjoyable drink, and this crusade proved unsuccessful.

Not long after George M. Jones's death in 1902, his widow Frances Watts Jones endowed a library in his memory. Erected just beyond Rivermont Bridge and built in the beaux-arts style, its construction expenditures eventually reached more than $100,000. Mrs. Jones also commissioned two nearly life-size bronze statues of her husband in a Confederate officer's uniform. These standing figures were by Solon H. Borglum, brother of the sculptor of Mount Rushmore, Gutzon Borglum. Jones thus became known to later generations as "General Jones," despite having only served in the Confederate ranks for about six months. One statue stands near Randolph-Macon's library; the other was for many years on the terrace of Jones Memorial Library, but is now at a Civil War–related site in Franklin County.

After some delays, the George M. Jones Memorial Library began full operations in June 1908. Though characterized by The *Lynchburg News* as a public facility, patronage was limited to white residents of Lynchburg, effectively barring African Americans and other minorities, non-resident college students (except at Randolph-Macon), and suburbanites beyond the city limits. These conditions remained until 1966, when a fully-integrated Lynchburg City Public Library opened in an older downtown building.

Stories abound about Mrs. Jones and her possessive attachment to the library that stood only a few hundred feet from her house. The librarians had to close the building and take their vacations when she chose to go out of town. On her frequent trips to the library, she supposedly rearranged its books according to colors. The staff would reshelf them in proper order after her departure. It has been said that even after Mrs. Jones's death librarians occasionally found books color-coded from red to black, indicating her desire to control the library extended beyond the grave.

In addition to a library, Lynchburg acquired a new performing arts center in the early twentieth century. Though an "Opera House" or "Academy of Music" was symbolic of the Victorian pursuit of high culture, these venues also hosted musicals, dances, comedic acts, lectures, and amateur theatricals. Lynchburg's 1879 Opera House had closed in 1903 and was converted to business use. The first guiding spirit for the Academy of Music was Richard D. Apperson, president of the Lynchburg Traction and Light Company, which ran electric streetcars and supplied electricity to private homes and businesses. Apperson and his partners purchased an old tobacco warehouse site at Sixth and Main Streets and within seven months the theatre was completed, opening on February 1, 1905.

The Academy enjoyed several successful seasons before it caught fire on April 20, 1911. Refurbished in beaux-arts style the following year under the leadership of C.M. Guggenheimer, who followed the ailing Apperson as president of the corporation, the Academy reopened in mid-December 1912 at the height of the social season. Under the guidance of local impresario Emma Adams, the Academy's pre–World

War I list of performers included violinists Efrem Zimbalist and Fritz Kreisler, singer Alma Gluck, humorist Will Rogers, and actors Douglas Fairbanks, John Drew, Maude Adams, and Ethel Barrymore. The city also had three movie houses by 1908, and by April 1913 the Academy screened short films.

1910 saw the death of five-term Senator John Warwick Daniel. "The Lame Lion of Virginia" had held a number of state and national offices in the Democratic party. Daniel ranked among Virginia's most famous sons from the 1880s until his death, and to honor him Lynchburg commissioned a larger-than-life seated statue paid for by public subscription. Curiously, the misfortunes of war seemed to follow Daniel; the delivery of his statue from Rome, where it had been sculpted by Sir Moses Ezekiel, was delayed by World War I.

In 1913, Lynchburg seemed poised on the brink of another economic renaissance. The city directory claimed that it was the third richest community in the United States. An extensive rail system, including the Chesapeake & Ohio, Southern, and the Norfolk and Western lines, offered travelers easy access to Washington, Atlanta, New Orleans, Chicago, and other points north and west. Lynchburg proclaimed itself as "the South's Shoe Center," and was strong in textile production, publishing, and banking.

In October the Hill City witnessed the arrival of the State Convention of Woman's Suffrage, hosted by the local Equal Suffrage League. Despite growing numbers of educated women, the struggle for voting rights continued to meet with indifferent success in Lynchburg. Although Orra Langhorne and a few kindred souls had founded the Virginia Suffrage Association in 1893, and the Equal Suffrage League was organized by Elizabeth Langhorne Lewis (a relative of Orra Langhorne by marriage) and five others in 1911, The *Lynchburg News* scornfully dismissed suffrage as a cause that did not "deserve to prevail" in the Old Dominion. In 1915, the League would have a membership of 204 women and 83 men. By that time the world was at war, a conflict into which all Americans, including central Virginians, would reluctantly be drawn in April 1917.

CHAPTER EIGHT

A SEASON OF STORMS
1914–1945

Lynchburg awoke to another summer morning on Sunday, June 28, 1914. There would be a church service for many, and then perhaps an afternoon of swimming at the YMCA Island, a picnic in one of the city's parks, or sitting in a rocker on the front porch watching the twilight descend. Life in the Hill City was good, and getting better every day. The following morning early risers were shocked to learn that the heir to the throne of Austria-Hungary and his wife had been assassinated by a Serbian-trained terrorist. In 1814 it would have taken six weeks for news to reach Lynchburg from the capitals of Europe; now it took less than 24 hours. While public sentiment condemned the murders of the Archduke and his wife, the story soon disappeared from the front page as other matters—like the July heat wave—attracted public attention.

"The Glorious Fourth" was celebrated with gusto, and then life slipped into its usual lazy summer pattern. Suddenly on July 23, the Austro-Hungarian ultimatum was presented to Serbia. It was rejected, and on July 28, the two nations were at war. Americans watched in disbelief as the complex system of alliances that had been constructed over the previous five decades sucked the great powers into the abyss. Only Britain hesitated, and then when Germany violated the 1839 treaty guaranteeing Belgian neutrality, London entered the war.

While news of the hostilities filled the local papers, inhabitants of central Virginia constantly reminded themselves that it was not their conflict. However, there were a number of recent immigrant residents who had ties to either one side or the other. Realizing the critical importance of the resources of the United States in a global struggle, the British were the first, and as time would prove, the most successful in exploiting the propaganda potential of the war. Initially troubled by Germany's abrogation of a long standing treaty, readers of The Lynchburg News were soon regaled by stories of German atrocities committed on the Belgian populace. Although Belgians in the Congo regularly mutilated African laborers who tried to escape their masters, American readers more readily accepted tales of Belgian boys having their right hands amputated to prevent their bearing arms against Germany. Allied cartoons and the designation of the Germans as "Huns" accelerated the process of changing public opinion.

Sheet music and records of songs like "It's a Long Long Way to Tipperary" and "Keep the Home Fires Burning" appeared in local shops, and boys whistled "Pack Up Your Troubles in Your Old Kit Bag" on their way to school. After all, Britain was our mother country, and France had helped us in our Revolution. By Christmas the war had become a stalemate, and the double line of trenches stretched from the English Channel to the Swiss border. Then on Friday, May 7, 1915, a German submarine sank the Cunard liner *Lusitania* and public opinion took another turn to the Allies.

Despite the risks, British passenger vessels continued to make the trans-Atlantic crossing after August 1914. The German government maintained that they were being used to ship strategic materials from the officially neutral United States to Great Britain. Both governments denied these allegations, but decades later the German charges were proven true. The *Lusitania* had been altered shortly after the war began to accommodate this contraband. When the *Lusitania* sank in 18 minutes after being hit by a torpedo from the U-20, it was not because of a design flaw as in the case of the RMS *Titanic*. The *Lusitania* was loaded with explosives. Twelve hundred men, women, and children drowned, and the disaster produced a firestorm in the American press. German-born citizens were accosted on the streets of Lynchburg, and their loyalty was questioned.

While former President Theodore Roosevelt demanded that the United States assume her place as a world power and come to the aid of the Allies, President Woodrow Wilson cautioned a more moderate course. Protests from the United States forced Germany to halt unrestricted submarine warfare. However, public opinion was now firmly against the Central Powers. By a strange twist of fate, a group of Lynchburg citizens were about to take the first steps towards their involvement in the Great War.

In 1915, Mexico was on the verge of a bloody civil war as General Pancho Villa launched a guerrilla campaign against the provisional government of President Carranza. In the melee, American citizens in Mexico were shot, and then Villa entered Texas and killed eight American soldiers and nine civilians. President Wilson's government reacted on March 10, 1916, by announcing that a special punitive expedition under General John J. "Black Jack" Pershing would be sent into Mexico to capture Villa. While the Pershing expedition was unsuccessful, it provided regulars and National Guard troops an excellent opportunity for in-the-field training. Many Lynchburgers were among their number.

The Lynchburg Home Guard, Company E, First Virginia Infantry, and a new organization, The Musketeers, Company L, First Virginia Infantry, were transported with other Virginia National Guard units to Brownsville, Texas. Returning early in 1917, the Guardsmen had only a brief respite. In addition to meddling in Mexican-American affairs, Germany had resumed unrestricted submarine warfare.

On April 2, President Wilson asked Congress for a declaration of war against the imperial German government. On April 4, the Senate approved the resolution. The Home Guard and the Musketeers were combined as Company L, 116th Infantry, 29th Division, and a new company, the Shawnee Rifles, was assigned to the 42nd Division. Before the Armistice was signed in November 1918, 2,500 Lynchburgers, most of them volunteers, served in the armed forces, and of that number 52 died. Their names were placed on two tablets on either side of the bronze sculpture, "The Listening Post," at the base of Monument Terrace created by the distinguished American sculptor, Charles Keck.

The number of service men who passed through Lynchburg on the way to various ports of embarkation was phenomenal. They were packed on the trains and provided with only the minimum amount of rations. Food and drinks offered by vendors along the way were sold at inflated prices, and most of the men in uniform could not afford to buy anything. When the men and women in charge of the Lynchburg Chapter of the Red Cross learned about this situation they organized canteens at both railway stations and provided plenty of food and hot coffee as troop trains made their brief stops. To thousands of men in uniform who fondly remembered it, Lynchburg literally became "Lunchburg."

The women of Lynchburg not only contributed countless hours to the Red Cross rolling bandages and making surgical dressings, they grew Victory Gardens, promoted Liberty Bonds and War Savings Stamps, and they filled the jobs in business and industry vacated when the men went off to the war. Although the Virginia General Assembly did not ratify the Nineteenth Amendment to the United States Constitution, a grateful nation finally recognized the sacrifice and service of America's women by granting them the right to vote in 1920.

The year America went to war, Lynchburg became the home of a new manufacturing plant that would vanish six years later. The Piedmont Motor Car Company produced a line of vehicles that were superb examples of modern design and engineering, but the fledgling firm could not compete with the giants of Detroit. The Piedmont models were more expensive than those, for example, manufactured by the Ford Motor Company, because all the parts used in assembling each model were not fabricated in Lynchburg. Although the company failed in the early 1920s, its cars quickly became popular with collectors, and every part of an old Piedmont is highly valued.

A Season of Storms: 1914–1945

In the late summer of 1918, as victory seemed a certainty, a new enemy, the "Spanish Influenza" struck the United States. Earlier in the year there had been a milder form of the influenza that affected an unusually high number of persons in Spain, hence the name. The virus that appeared later in the year was a deadly mutation of the earlier strain. The pandemic lasted only a few weeks, but before it ended, the estimated world-wide death toll was 40 million. To avoid a panic, many municipal authorities chose not to issue any information on the disease and the bizarre rumors that swirled about it. This lack of information actually created hysteria in many communities. The majority of victims were seemingly healthy men and women in the prime of life; the military camps were particularly affected. Those who survived the influenza often died from pneumonia.

In Lynchburg there was neither panic nor hysteria, thanks in large part to the efforts of two men: Mayor Royston Jester Jr. and Dr. Mosby G. Perrow, the City Health Officer. From the appearance of the first case in the city they were completely open with the public; no information on the nationwide progress of the disease was withheld from the press. The *Lynchburg News* was filled with stories related to the outbreak, as well as instructions on how to deal with this new killer. Together the citizens of Lynchburg faced this deadly enemy. Although an estimated 250 died before the end of the pandemic, many more might have succumbed had it not been for the tireless efforts of Dr. Perrow, his fellow physicians, and the members of the nursing community, as well as the complete support of Mayor Jester and city council. The number of deaths began to decline as news reached Lynchburg of the armistice signed on November 11, and by Christmas the influenza was fast fading from public memory.

As the Versailles Peace Conference drew to a close in June 1919, President Wilson was forced to compromise on most of his "Fourteen Points" to save the League of Nations. The final result was a punitive treaty against the defeated Central Powers. Since 1918, Lynchburg native Carter Glass had been Wilson's Secretary of the Treasury, and he firmly supported the League. He tried to use his influence with his former colleagues in the Senate to secure its passage, but to no avail. Both the Treaty of Versailles and the Charter of the League were rejected.

In 1913, as a member of the House Banking and Currency Committee, Glass co-sponsored the Federal Reserve Act with Robert Latham Owen, another Lynchburg native, then senator from Oklahoma. In 1837, Andrew Jackson had destroyed the Bank of the United States for political reasons and produced economic chaos; the Federal Reserve restored that stability and in time proved to be one of the most important pieces of legislation of the twentieth century. In 1920, Glass moved from

LYNCHBURG

the House to the Senate to fill the unexpired term of the late Thomas S. Martin, his political adversary. Glass would remain in the Senate until his own death in 1946. Although he was a lifelong Democrat, Glass would prove an implacable foe of Franklin D. Roosevelt's New Deal.

As the veterans of the Great War returned home and began to resume their interrupted careers, the citizens of Lynchburg chose to alter the way in which the city was administered. In 1920 the mayoral form of government, with its bicameral council, was replaced by a council of five members and a city manager form of municipal government. The sometimes chaotic, but always exciting course of local politics now gave way to an oligarchy that was efficient, honest, and often boring. A council of five representing a population of over 30,000 was considered too elitist by many citizens, but it was not until 1928 that the Virginia General Assembly saw fit to increase the number to seven. Although in theory the members of council represented the entire population of the city, for the next 50 years they were, for the most part, white upper-middle class.

The 1920s, like the 1820s, was a time of growth and prosperity for the Hill City. Monument Terrace was constructed between 1924 and 1925 as a monument to the local soldiers who died in the Great War, but its appearance was altered a year later when the dolphin fountain was replaced by "The Listening Post." The physical appearance of Lynchburg had already been transformed by the completion of the Williams Viaduct in 1918. Within a few years the Fifth Street Viaduct, D Street Bridge, and the encasement of the old steel and wooden Rivermont Bridge in concrete were finished, facilitating street car travel to all parts of the city. Much to the regret of many citizens the streetcars would be replaced by a fleet of buses in 1941, with many of the tracks being removed and donated to the war effort.

In 1926, the year that Rivermont Bridge was refurbished, Lynchburg completed the tenth annexation of county land in its history. This increase in the city's tax base allowed an improvement in services. The "new" citizens were able to take advantage of one of the best school systems in Virginia. They also had access to the largest shopping area in central Virginia. Most of the department stores and smaller shops were locally owned. The quality of restaurants and hotels was equal to cities twice Lynchburg's size, as were the public and private recreation facilities—swimming pools, golf courses, and athletic fields—available to most white residents.

Like many American cities, Lynchburg was a completely racially segregated community. The fiction of "separate but equal" was the accepted order. Public transportation, education, entertainment, leisure activities, and recreation were separate, but in most cases not identical. Talented and ambitious black men and women who might have enriched the quality of life in Lynchburg had no choice before the mid-1960s but to leave their birthplace for an environment more accepting of their race. Thus they became part of the migration of 1.5 million southern blacks to northern cities between 1919 and 1929.

It is ironic that even in memory the heroic dead of World War I are separated. The names of black soldiers were divided from their white comrades on the tablets at the base of Monument Terrace. During the city's bicentennial celebration it was suggested that the tablets be replaced and the names be placed in alphabetical order without regard to race. However, it was decided to leave them untouched as a reminder of the inequalities of the past and a warning to future generations to always be on guard against prejudice.

In the 1920s, the Academy of Music Theatre under the management of Roland Hamner brought a galaxy of stars to Lynchburg's finest auditorium. A young Bob Hope, who was playing the Trenton Theater at the corner of Main and Eleventh Streets, supposedly stood in the wings of the Academy one afternoon in the early 1920s and watched Will Rogers lasso the audience with his one-liners. Years later in 1977, Hope, now a legend in the world of entertainment, returned to Lynchburg to play in a charity golf tournament. As he drove through downtown he asked his host to stop by the Academy, now deserted, for a moment so he could savor a very pleasant memory.

Richard Doty, long the "guardian spirit" of the Academy, loved to tell this story to everyone who visited the theater, even showing them where Hope stood, but unfortunately this urban legend is not genuine. The only time Hope and Rogers performed in Lynchburg at the same time was early in December 1925. Bob Hope was indeed on the bill at the Trenton, but Will Rogers was at the City Auditorium, not the Academy. Hope might have caught part of Rogers's act, but there is no way of verifying this. In 1977 he may well have stopped by the Academy, but unfortunately he probably never was in the theater. However, the stories about spirits and the stars are true.

In 2001, workmen were checking the soundness of the supports of the main auditorium and uncovered a cache of liquor bottles. Some were empty, others were partly filled, and some had never been opened. On October 18, 1919, the Volstead Act was passed, and their interment probably coincided with the early months of Prohibition. Happy Billy's Saloon was just across the street from the Academy and between the acts men regularly patronized it; thus there was no reason for bottles to be buried in the basement. Or was there?

The managers of the Academy prided themselves on bringing quality entertainment to Lynchburg, and thus they were expected to cater to the whims of the stars who appeared on stage between 1905 and 1920. Some performers required that an unopened bottle of their favorite libation be waiting in their dressing room for a "bit of courage" before the performance, or a longer drink after the final curtain. While these perks might not be included in the formal contract, they were expected nonetheless. The agent who confirmed the engagement informed the manager of his client's tastes, and of when the refreshments were required.

From 1905 until 1920, a rather varied collection of empty, partially consumed, and unopened bottles must have collected in the manager's office closet. When Prohibition was first enforced, he had already purchased bottles for the performers who were engaged for the new season. To avoid the embarrassing task of explaining the "collection" to the authorities, Mr. Hamner eventually buried the bottles in the basement in the hope that the Volstead Act would soon be repealed and life would return to normal. By the time Prohibition was abolished, the Academy was a movie theater under new management, and the "stash" in the basement was forgotten. Some of the bottles will be permanently displayed in the proposed museum of theater in Lynchburg to be housed in the restored Academy of Fine Arts. One cannot help but speculate—did Evelyn Nesbit Thaw demand champagne, and if so, did she drain the contents after performing on her red velvet swing? There are a couple of bottles that once contained "the bubbly." Were they for her?

In its "Silver Decade" Lynchburg acquired most of the trappings of a prosperous sophisticated urban center. Civic clubs and fraternal organizations abounded for both races. White amateur artists and actors had almost unlimited opportunities to develop their talents in the Lynchburg Art Club and the Lynchburg Little Theater. Two country clubs, Oakwood and Boonsboro, provided tennis, golf, swimming, and social activities, again for affluent whites. Modern cities also must have a skyscraper, and so in 1929, the same year that city council authorized the construction of Preston Glenn Field in memory of a local pilot who died in the Great War, the foundation of the Allied Arts Building was poured. Two years later, in the depth of the Depression, this handsome Art-Deco structure was completed—a constant reminder of the world that vanished on "Black Thursday," October 24, 1929.

The determined efforts of the post–Civil War business community to increase the economic diversity of Lynchburg were vindicated as the city managed to avoid severe economic deterioration during the Great Depression. Throughout a long decade of recovery the Lynchburg Chamber of Commerce continued to tirelessly market the economic stability of the Hill City and, like their nineteenth-century predecessors, they were remarkably successful. Their task was made somewhat easier by the fact that none of the financial institutions in Lynchburg failed during the Depression. For two generations Lynchburgers faithfully did business with "Mr. Tom Gilliam's bank," "Mr. Jim Gilliam's bank," or one of the smaller firms that handled the city's money.

Although the members of city council were dedicated to fiscal conservatism, they were also tempted by the largesse that cascaded from the federal coffers after Franklin Delano Roosevelt became president in March 1933. He promised a "New Deal" for the American people, and during the first 100 days of his administration measures that transformed the country poured from the halls of Congress. Loathing government interference in local affairs, even more than newfangled inventions like the telephone, Senator Carter Glass fought Roosevelt and his legislation every step of the way, but his was a losing battle.

Lynchburg was luckier than many communities because most of its factories and stores were still locally owned; thus the proprieters tried very hard to prevent closures and to mitigate the inevitable reduction of wages and the loss of jobs. Their employees were often their neighbors and friends. Many of the men and women who faced unemployment had held positions with firms whose home offices were far from Lynchburg. Because of its extensive rail system, Lynchburg was like a magnet to the homeless men who wandered from one place to another looking for work. Late in 1933, the city created a shelter for them in an old warehouse; then early in the new year, in the midst of one of the coldest winters on record, tragedy struck. A grease fire in the Transient Bureau's kitchen spread rapidly through the old building, and the men who were trapped on the upper floors panicked. The dead numbered 22 and the injured exceeded 70. The Transient Bureau fire forced city leaders to accept federal assistance to prevent a similar disaster in the future.

By 1936, when Lynchburg celebrated its Sesquicentennial, the city's economic recovery was well advanced. The month of October was devoted to the festivities, and the city's hotels were filled with visitors and many who returned to their hometown to celebrate its birthday.

One of the most important sources of funding for the celebration was the sale of a special half dollar struck by the United States Mint in Philadelphia. Lynchburg and Norfolk are the only Virginia cities honored with a commemorative coin. There were 16 commemorative half dollars struck in 1936 with an average mintage of 32,263. The Lynchburg coin, designed by Charles Keck, featured Miss Liberty and Monument Terrace on the reverse, and a profile portrait of Carter Glass on the obverse.

The Senator had objected, but President Roosevelt had insisted, and vanity finally triumphed. It was obviously an attempt to win Glass's support for the next phase of the New Deal, but it failed. When Lynchburg's Sesquicentennial Committee sought the striking of more halves—the final total was only 20,013—their request was denied by the Secretary of the Treasury. Five pre-1936 commemoratives were re-struck that year with an average mintage of 27,025; thus Lynchburg's request was not an unusual one. Obviously Carter Glass was not for sale, although he was the first living American to appear alone on the obverse of a commemorative coin.

Critics of the New Deal often accused President Roosevelt of reacting to each crisis without having a well-defined plan for recovery. That same appraisal might on occasion be applied to the Lynchburg City Council, because they had no master plan, and at times they overreacted to a local emergency. However, city leaders somehow found a balance between independence and federal assistance, and by the end of the 1930s municipal finances were in good condition. Lynchburg's credit rating was excellent, because the city never failed to meet its obligations while many municipalities of comparable size were declaring bankruptcy.

During the Great Depression Americans concentrated on their own problems, and often ignored events in other parts of the world that were shaping their future. The local papers did not fail to report the expansion of the Empire of Japan into China, or chronicle the rise of Benito Mussolini in Italy and Adolph Hitler in Germany; and their editorial pages were filled with speculation on what all this might mean for America. However, it was not until Germany's invasion of Poland on September 1, 1939, and the declaration of war by Great Britain and France two days later, when Americans began to consider that they might be sucked into another world conflict. The sympathies of most lay with the Allies, and various charities began to raise funds and purchase supplies for the beleaguered British and French, despite the government's overt stance of strict neutrality.

After the fall of France in June 1940, President Roosevelt used his skills as a politician to ease the restrictions of the various Neutrality Acts through the Lend-Lease Acts that benefited Britain, and later the Soviet Union. In September 1940, the Selective Service and Training Act was passed. All able-bodied men between 21 and 35 were required to register, but many considered that to be only a precautionary measure. Then on Sunday, December 7, 1941, isolationism and neutrality ended with the Japanese attack on Pearl Harbor. The next day the United States declared war on Japan. On December 11, Germany and Italy went to war with the United States.

A week after the declaration of war, city council approved the creation of the Lynchburg Defense Unit, which soon became the Lynchburg Civil Defense Corps. Although Lynchburg was never a target for enemy aircraft, there were regular blackouts supervised by a number of air-raid wardens. Before the war ended, there were over 3,000 men and women working as volunteers to keep the city safe and operating normally. Since many of Lynchburg's industries produced items essential to the war effort, they were protected from possible sabotage with guards, barriers, barbed wire, and numerous security checks.

The city was also designated as an evacuation site for coastal areas in case of invasion. The governmental units—national, state, and local—were taking no chances. Works of art from the museums in Washington were evacuated to a number of sites, including Randolph-Macon Woman's College. It already had an exceptional collection of modern works purchased under the supervision of art professor Louise Jordan Smith. The college collection, along with the evacuated works, eventually formed the core of what became the Maier Museum, one of Lynchburg's most valued assets.

In the spring of 1942, and every year thereafter until the war ended, every piece of available arable ground was devoted to Victory Gardens. The produce from these patches was either canned or offered for sale in the city market, or in local grocery stores. The first item to be rationed was sugar, followed by other foods including meats, canned fruits, and coffee. There was some inevitable hoarding, but for the most part citizens of Lynchburg did their part by consuming only their fair share of strictly rationed items.

One of the lighter moments during the war occurred in January 1942. Rebecca Yancy Williams had published an affectionate and often humorous memoir of her father, Captain Bob Yancy, Lynchburg's colorful commonwealth's attorney. *The Vanishing Virginian* was made into a film, and its world premier was held at the Paramount Theater, Lynchburg's newest movie palace. Frank Morgan, the popular character actor who had played the Wizard of Oz, easily turned his talents to portraying the cantankerous and sometimes profane "Capin Bob." The whole event was a complete success as the local gentry arrived in style to mingle with some of Hollywood's finest. The next morning it was business as usual, but for one brief evening Hitler and Tojo, Japan's wartime commander, were forgotten.

In World War I, Lynchburg had been dubbed "Lunchburg;" now it became a "liberty town." Soldiers from Camp Pickett, near Blackstone, regularly spent their weekend passes in Lynchburg. The government had created the United Services Organization (USO) in December 1941, and the city quickly requested that a unit be formed in Lynchburg. The Red Cross and local citizens also offered hospitality for the servicemen. The military authorities attempted to restrict contact between servicemen and those young women who carried on the tradition of the Buzzard, but they were unsuccessful. The center for such activities had moved from the banks of the James to an area centered around Fourth Street, called "the Hill." During the war years young men in borrowed civilian attire supplied through a third party regularly avoided the military police.

Most of the time the service personnel who visited Lynchburg during the war behaved themselves. At Christmas 1942, 5,000 soldiers from Camp Pickett were invited to spend the holiday with local families. It was a bittersweet celebration for some of their hosts because many of their sons and daughters were also in uniform and far from home, being entertained by strangers. Each Thanksgiving and Christmas until the end of the war many Lynchburg homes were opened to servicemen and women.

During the first year of the war the local draft board had little to do because Lynchburg supplied its quotas with volunteers. As the men went off to war women filled their jobs, and for many this was the beginning of a lifelong career. Children did their part too by collecting paper, scrap metal, edible fats, and anything else that could be used for the war effort. Lynchburgers actually collected more scrap metal per capita—over 300 pounds—than any other city in the country. They also excelled at selling war bonds, and as a result of their efforts a bomber was named *The City of Lynchburg*. The plane survived the war, and like so many similar craft was decommissioned after 1945 and vanished. On May 1, 1943, it was announced that men from 38 to 45 were subject to being drafted. Three months later ten percent of the city's population, both men and women, were in uniform. Throughout the war Lynchburgers made sure that members of the various armed services were not forgotten. Cards, letters, cookies, and candy packed in popcorn, mittens, socks, scarves, and the Christmas boxes filled by the Jaycees were vital links between home and the front.

On June 6, 1944, the news for which the free world had waited so long was announced on the radio and in banner headlines; Hitler's "Fortress Europe" had been breached. The price paid for D-Day was high, particularly for nearby Bedford, Virginia. Rare indeed was a family in that tiny community not touched by the tragedy. Nineteen young men out of a total population of 3,200 fell at Normandy. Proportionally, if Lynchburg had lost the same percentage of its servicemen, the number would be 263; and for New York it would be approximately 4,500. The National D-Day Memorial in Bedford, dedicated on June 6, 2001, by President George W. Bush, is a reminder of their sacrifice. When Lynchburg celebrated Armistice Day on November 11, 1944, the names of 100 servicemen who had already lost their lives were listed on temporary tablets at the base of Monument Terrace next to their comrades who had fallen in World War I.

By the beginning of 1945 it was obvious that the war was entering its final phase. The Allied victory in the Battle of the Bulge marked the beginning of the end for Nazi

Germany, and the fall of each Japanese-held island numbered the days of the Empire of the Rising Sun. Then on April 12, President Roosevelt died in Warm Springs, Georgia, from a cerebral hemorrhage. It was a cool crisp spring dawn when his funeral train passed through Lynchburg. The crowd at the Kemper Street station was large and silent. White citizens stood side by side with black; children, their parents, the elderly, the infirm all watched the last car with its flag-draped coffin—each corner guarded by a member of a different branch of the services—move slowly through the station. There was not a sound, save the clatter of the wheels and the song of the birds greeting the new morning. The war in Europe ended the following month, and in August the Japanese surrendered. World War II was finished. Lynchburg's sons and daughters were coming home.

CHAPTER NINE

A SOCIETY OF FRIENDS

1945–1977

On May 28, 1946, Senator Carter Glass died, but outside his native Lynchburg few noticed his passing. Because of ill health he had been unable to fulfill his legislative duties during the last years of his life. Since he refused to resign, Virginia was represented by only one senator until the death of Glass. The world that he embodied had already vanished at Pearl Harbor, Anzio, and on the beaches at Normandy.

With the end of the war and the return of the veterans, Lynchburg looked forward to growth and prosperity, but it did not come. The bright future predicted by so many during the years of conflict initially seemed to bypass Lynchburg. There was not a second great depression as some had foretold, and in time there was real growth in unexpected places.

Beginning in the fall of 1942, the student body at Lynchburg College began to shrink until the classrooms were almost empty because every able-bodied male student either volunteered or was drafted. Dr. Riley B. Montgomery arranged with the government to make the campus available for training air force cadets, and that ensured the survival of the college until the end of hostilities. Even the most optimistic members of the faculty and administration could not have imagined what happened in the fall of 1945 when the Class of 1949 matriculated. Suddenly there were veterans in almost every class. When the full effects of the G.I. Bill of Rights were felt the following year, the college seemed to be bursting at the seams. Josephus and Sarah LaRue Hopwood's little experiment on the edge of Lynchburg had finally come into its own.

Between 1945 and 1950, $15 billion in federal funds was pumped into the nation's economy, thanks to the Serviceman's Readjustment Act of 1944—the G.I. Bill's official name—and with Lynchburg College's resurgence city businesses began to revive from the economic doldrums and receive their fair share of the federal bounty. However, this legislation still worried a number of the more conservative city leaders. After all, this was a New Deal measure initiated by "Franklin Deficit Roosevelt" and promulgated by the new president, Harry S Truman, both political enemies of the late Senator Carter Glass.

Unfortunately for the city, most of the graduates from the post-war classes sought careers far beyond the limits of Lynchburg. Of course some of them remained in central Virginia, but most did not. Before World War II, higher education had been the domain of a very small proportion of the general population. With the G.I. Bill, students from a socio-economic group that was almost devoid of college graduates in 1900 could aspire to careers once reserved for the privileged. Viewed as a nationwide trend, within 25 years this leveling process would alter the political power structure of the Hill City.

Lynchburg College produced a number of elementary and secondary school teachers, and to obtain certification from the state of Virginia they were required to complete a program of student teaching. However, the city schools were closed to student teachers from Lynchburg College unless there was not a student from Randolph-Macon Woman's College to fill a particular teaching slot. Lynchburg College students were forced to complete their required preparation in the schools of Martinsville, Virginia. This inconvenience continued until 1961 when Dr. Lester Carper replaced Dr. Paul Munro as the superintendent of the city schools. At times Lynchburg seemed as suspicious of change as it had 50 or 75 years earlier, but with the pace of life quickening throughout America in the mid-twentieth century, maintaining the status quo became increasingly difficult.

Another group of citizens who were changed by the war were African Americans, who had been a silent, almost invisible minority since they were disenfranchised at the turn of the century. They had done their part on the home front, and had shed their blood in defense of freedom and equality, and now they demanded their share of both. The hour of their deliverance was at hand, and it was the federal government that took the lead in making the words of the Declaration of Independence ring true. In July 1948, President Truman desegregated the armed forces and won re-election that November, in spite of the defection of the States Rights Democrats, or "Dixiecrats," led by J. Strom Thurman of South Carolina. Antebellum politics had no place in a Cold War world.

In 1950, Lynchburg took the first steps to building a new E.C. Glass High School, a project that had been discussed since the late 1930s. That same summer the United Nations became embroiled in the Korean War and, as in the past, Lynchburg made its human and material contributions to this new struggle. In 1952 Virginia voted Republican for the first time since 1928 and, as white students were preparing to enter their new high school in the fall of 1953, President Dwight D. Eisenhower brought an end to the war in Korea.

While Supreme Commander of the Allied forces in Europe during World War II, Eisenhower had the opportunity to examine the Autobahn, one of the most successful building projects undertaken by the Third Reich. When he became

LYNCHBURG

President, Eisenhower successfully promoted a legislative initiative to provide the United States with a similar scheme: the Interstate Highway System. In the original design, Lynchburg was scheduled to be linked to Norfolk and Richmond by Interstate 64, but this did not come to pass. In 1952 Lynchburg helped to elect Richard Poff, a Republican, to the House of Representatives. Thus when President John F. Kennedy later altered the route of I-64 to pass through Charlottesville instead of Lynchburg to satisfy the request of one of his political cronies, there was not a Democrat in Congress willing to speak for the needs of the Hill City.

Kennedy did not foresee or care about the long-term effects upon the economic future of central Virginia. As the only major city in the commonwealth without an interstate connection, Lynchburg has missed a number of opportunities to attract new industries to the city, and it has been unable to prevent some firms from leaving. Some citizens, trying to make the best of an unfortunate situation, maintain that they never really wanted an interstate connection in the first place, but this is mere equivocation. Over the years various schemes have been advanced for expanding the interstate system to include Lynchburg, but so far they have not materialized.

For the most part Lynchburgers liked Eisenhower's dynamic conservatism, but on May 17, 1954, they were not prepared for the Supreme Court's discarding the doctrine of separate but equal in the famous *Brown vs. Board of Education of Topeka* decision. A century after the citizens of Lynchburg had struggled with the question of secession, they faced the equally traumatic problem of integration. This time they made the right choice, and help came from an unexpected quarter.

In 1950 the economic health of Lynchburg seemed to be based on the same industries—shoes and textiles—that had sparked its recovery from the Civil War, and the renewal of stiff foreign competition promised a bleak future. Then on March 8, 1955, it was announced that one of the leaders in the new nuclear industry, Babcock and Wilcox, would build a plant at Mount Athos in Campbell County. The fact that the Lynchburg area would soon contain more enriched uranium than any other site in the country did not seem to bother anyone. Six months later, on September 23, 1955, General Electric announced its intention to build a huge plant in the city. In time Babcock and Wilcox would merge with the giant French firm, Framatome, and the Swedish firm Ericsson would purchase General Electric, allowing it to slowly vanish. In 1955 all this lay far in the future; Lynchburg was on the verge of another economic boom.

Most of the senior staff for both of these firms were transferred from installations in the North and Midwest, where labor troubles were endemic. Moving to Virginia, a right-to-work state, was a wonderful opportunity, and landing in

A Society of Friends: 1945–1977

Lynchburg, where real worker unrest belonged in the 1880s, became an added bonus. Some local writers have referred to their relocation as "the second Northern invasion," and others have unkindly referred to them as "spoilers." Migration is a better description for their resettlement, and catalyst a more accurate delineation of their vital role in the city's history.

Lynchburg avoided the violence and polarization that threatened many Southern communities during the desegregation crisis of the 1950s and the 1960s. This was due to a combination of factors: the conservatism and good sense of the "old guard," the black churches and the fraternal organizations' decision to follow the path of reason and non-violence, and also the influx of new citizens who worked a subtle transformation in the white population in less than a decade.

The new industries' managers, engineers, and their families slowly moved to Lynchburg, and for a time they remained clustered together socially; then gradually—but with purpose—they became part of local churches, civic organizations, heritage groups, and country clubs. Their daughters became debutantes and members of the Spinster German as they entered Hollins, Sweet Briar, and Randolph-Macon Woman's College. Their sons matriculated to William and Mary, Washington and Lee, and Virginia Military Institute. They were the moving force behind the Virginia Ten Miler, and they revitalized the Republican Party in Lynchburg. Suddenly it was fashionable not to be a Democrat. Far more important was the subtle, subliminal way that the newcomers changed attitudes towards race and ethnic diversity. Without them Lynchburg might have repeated the ordeal of 1865–1870. Many of them are gone now, but their legacy will last far into the twenty-first century.

While communities around Lynchburg closed their public schools and precipitated a crisis in education whose effects are still apparent, the city remained deceptively calm. Then on December 14, 1960, six college students—two from Lynchburg College, two from Randolph-Macon Woman's College, and two from Virginia Seminary and College—decided to attempt to integrate the lunch counter at Patterson's Drug Store on Main Street. Their sit-in caught both the black and white communities by surprise, and their actions landed them in court and finally in jail, but they gave new impetus to the civil rights movement in the Hill City.

On July 4, 1961, there was an attempt to integrate Miller Park Pool, but it only led to the closing of all of the city's public pools, both black and white. In 1976 a new Miller Park Pool would open, the city council's bicentennial gift to Lynchburg, but for 15 summers those persons who did not have a membership at one of the country clubs had only the river or the kindness of people like the Reverend Beverly

Cosby of the Church of the Covenant off Boonsboro Road. The Lodge of the Fisherman on the grounds of the church became a gathering place for those who wished to transform their city. Hoping to close this conduit for change, conservative city authorities forbade the staff of the Lodge to charge for the food and beverages they served because they did not have a restaurant license. They could only suggest a price. Many came and refused to pay for their meals; many others came and willingly paid twice. The Lodge of the Fisherman survived.

Owen Cardwell and Lynda Woodruff became the first African-American students to enroll at E.C. Glass High School on January 29, 1962. Two months later, Dr. Martin Luther King Jr. spoke to an integrated capacity audience in the E.C. Glass Auditorium. Like so many leaders of the black community before him, he also visited Anne Spencer in her Pierce Street home.. A plethora of plans to slow the progress of integration were presented to the Lynchburg School Board, but they would all be rejected. It was not an easy task, and at times tempers on both sides flared almost to the flash point, but in the end common sense prevailed. Haltingly, Lynchburg took the first real steps to becoming a truly united community. One indication of this new spirit in the Hill City was the complete failure of the Klu Klux Klan to organize a rally in the city in the summer of 1966.

In 1968 Dr. Fred Young became superintendent of schools and before he left Lynchburg three years later he had devised a workable desegregation plan that included busing children from inner city neighborhoods to previously all-white schools. Since that time, more than a generation of children has been reared in Lynchburg for whom the concept of segregation seems as antiquated as the feudal system. The one tragedy in this story of progress was the demolition in 1979 of Dunbar High School, long the symbol of African-American pride and success. Tremendous progress in improving race relations has been made in Lynchburg since the end of World War II, but much remains to be done. However, every time friends from different races join each other for a meal in a local restaurant, exercise together at a Lynchburg gym, worship together, or enjoy a cultural program at a city venue, another victory is won. Our Quaker founders would be pleased but conscious of the work that still needs to be done.

One of the post–war phenomena that affected almost all urban centers in the United States was the slow decay of the inner city, and Lynchburg was not immune to this trend. In 1945 with gasoline rationing at an end, America's love affair with the internal combustion engine began anew. In January of that year the streets of Lynchburg were almost devoid of motor vehicles; by January 1946 they were congested, especially Commerce, Main, Church, and Court Streets. Making Main and Church Streets one way did little to alleviate the problem. Then in 1959, the opening of Pittman Plaza on Memorial Avenue seemed to deal a deathblow to downtown Lynchburg. The closure of the Academy Theater the previous year appeared like the prologue to another urban tragedy. One by one the stores that had been the life blood of early twentieth century Main Street began to close or move their operations to the new shopping center with its ample free parking.

The opening of the Lynchburg Fine Arts Center in 1962, and the construction of a new Lynchburg General Hospital, both within walking distance of Pittman Plaza, seemed to indicate that the city's center was shifting to the west towards Preston Glenn Field, soon to be renamed Lynchburg Municipal Airport. As the shopping center replaced the city center, so the airplane began to replace the passenger train as the preferred method of long-distance travel. Americans seemed to be constantly on the move, and the faster the better.

The citizens of Lynchburg, like their counterparts all over the country, were moving from old, long-established neighborhoods into the suburbs. As residents left the inner city, many elegant homes on Diamond Hill, Federal Hill, Courthouse Hill, and Daniel's Hill were converted into small, cramped apartments often owned by absentee landlords who were interested only in quick profits, and did not hesitate to charge exorbitant rents for substandard housing. Slowly the city's magnificent architectural heritage began to decay. At the same time numerous structures from Lynchburg's past vanished to satisfy the seemingly insatiable hunger for parking lots, service stations, branch banks, and convenience stores.

Yet while the city's inner core seemed to be decaying, it was actually evolving. In 1966 the Lynchburg City Library opened in an old downtown warehouse. Although there had been a century's worth of discussion about a public library for Lynchburg, this was the first facility that served all citizens as well as our neighbors in the surrounding counties. This was another example of the positive involvement of families that had moved to Lynchburg to work at Babcock and Wilcox and General Electric. They galvanized public interest in a new library, and then played a vital role in planning the facility. In 1984 it moved into the old Sears building at Pittman Plaza. Its original home was then demolished to expand a multi-leveled parking lot constructed by the city.

Another college was added to Lynchburg's roster of institutions of higher learning in 1967. Central Virginia Community College is part of the state system of two-year institutions created to serve as bridges between public high school and senior colleges. The first classes at CVCC were held in temporary quarters in downtown Lynchburg, and there were many who hoped that this would become a permanent arrangement, thus stimulating the revitalization of the city's core. However, it was determined by state and local authorities that CVCC would be located on a new campus to be built on the southern edge of the city near Wards Road, since there was more room there for future expansion.

Another turning point in Lynchburg's renewal occurred the following year when the restoration of Point of Honor became the ambitious project of the newly organized Lynchburg Historical Foundation Incorporated, and the Academy of Music Theatre was saved from possible demolition. Both events are indicative of a rediscovery and a renewed appreciation by the community of its architectural heritage. However, it took a decade to complete the first project, and the latter effort is still in development. Lynchburg has never embraced rapid change of any kind, even when it involves saving the echoes of its past.

Dr. George Cabell's mansion house on the bluff overlooking the point where Blackwater Creek joins the James River was once the center of a vast estate. Whether the point of land below the house was the site of "affairs of honor" is debatable, but nevertheless it has become a cherished local legend. Built around 1815, Point of Honor remained a private residence until 1928, when it became a community center and playground. Forty years of minimal maintenance and daily wear reduced the house to the rather shabby state from which the foundation rescued it. The restoration was funded by both private and public monies, in particular a bequest from the estate of Katherine Diggs. Point of Honor was adopted as part of the Lynchburg Museum System in 1976. Its grounds and gardens became a project of the Garden Club of Virginia the following year. The addition of a carriage house and an early nineteenth-century kitchen have transformed Point of Honor once again into a showplace of which the city may be justly proud. It is a favored destination for tourists from all over the commonwealth and the eastern United States.

That same year, 1968, rumors began to circulate throughout the city that VDOT (the Virginia Department of Transportation) intended to replace the Williams Viaduct with a new bridge. The plan involved a reconfiguration of the access to Fifth Street, with the new route to pass through the Academy of Music Theatre. The threat of demolition energized a group of citizens led by the sisters Lib and Virginia Wiley, and the indomitable Dr. Roberta D. Cornelius, Professor of English at Randolph-Macon Woman's College. She even threatened to chain herself to the doors of the theatre if one brick was harmed. That did not prove necessary; the Friends of the Academy of Music Theater saved the building and began to raise money and gain public support for the return of the Beaux Arts classic to its former glory. It was the first building in the city to be placed on the National Register of Historic Places as well as the Virginia Landmarks Register. Unfortunately the recession of the 1970s and later rampant inflation prevented the completion of the project. The building was saved and stabilized, but not refurbished.

In 1970 Lynchburg lost one of its architectural treasures and the original building at Lynchburg College, Westover Hall. There had been plans advanced since the early 1920s to either remodel or raze this wooden version of Chambord, but Dr. M. Carey Brewer, the young and energetic president of the college, actually ordered the demolition in the summer of 1970. A number of reasons, or—in the eyes of some alumni—excuses were advanced for this action, but in actuality Westover simply did not fit into the developmental scheme of the college administration. However, it has never really been replaced, either physically or in the hearts of alumni.

The Reverend Jerry Falwell had founded Thomas Road Baptist Church in a deserted soft drink plant in 1956. Since then the church has enjoyed phenomenal growth in large part because of the charismatic Falwell, who is a native son. His nationally syndicated "Old Time Gospel Hour" is viewed each week by millions worldwide. Because of its pastor's high visibility, the church over the years has provided a popular venue for a number of the more prominent figures of the Christian right, as well as conservative politicians.

Fifteen years after the founding of Thomas Road Baptist Church, Lynchburg Baptist College opened its doors with 154 students. Its name was changed in 1976 to Liberty Baptist College to avoid confusion with nearby Lynchburg College and to mark the nation's bicentennial. As a result of continued growth and the expansion of its programs, its name was changed again to Liberty University in 1985. As with the other colleges in the area, Liberty University has generated handsome profits for Lynchburg businesses and convinced many local leaders that the city's future wealth lies in tourism and higher education, not industry. Attracted by its relative security and its comparatively moderate cost of living, many parents, particularly from the Northeast, have sent their sons and daughters to be educated in the Hill City's eight colleges. Lynchburg has become the temporary home of students from every state in the Union and nations all over the world.

Virginia, Great Britain's first colony in North America, has retained the system of independent counties and cities imported to the commonwealth in the seventeenth century. In other states, counties and cities form one political unit, thus avoiding the bitter quarrels that have marred the relationship between Virginia's urban centers and the counties they border. In order to survive cities must grow, and in Virginia this means annexation. Lynchburg completed its first successful incursion into county territory in 1805, and since then countless acres from Bedford and Campbell counties have been added to the city. However, no attempt to annex caused as much controversy as the resolution passed by city council on January 29, 1972. Two years later the city received half of the land it sought, with seven square miles from Bedford County and 18 square miles from Campbell County. This annexation polarized the political factions in the city and led to the ouster of all but one of the incumbents in the very next councilmanic election.

Defeat was a word that haunted America's collective subconscious in the early 1970s as the Vietnam War ground to a less than glorious end. When the nation's involvement in southeast Asia began in President Eisenhower's administration, most Americans knew very little about the former French colony of Indochina that had split into two parts after it achieved independence. Once again, as in Korea, the democratic South faced the communist North, but this was an entirely different conflict. As the war escalated, so did the protests at home against it—particularly on college campuses. Lynchburg was not immune to the antiwar movement. Lynchburg College, Randolph-Macon Woman's College, Sweet Briar, CVCC, and Virginia Seminary and College all witnessed protests, but they were subdued compared to other campuses. Only Liberty Baptist College seemed free of the demonstrations and petitions. There were also public protests at Monument Terrace, which pitted members of the peace movement against veterans of earlier wars. A number of young men and women from Lynchburg served in the war; some never came home, while others were shattered by their experiences as prisoners. When the Vietnam debacle finally ended, Lynchburg tried to forget it by focusing on the two-hundredth anniversary of the founding of the Republic.

As the bicentennial of the founding of the United States approached, support grew in Lynchburg for the creation of historic districts to protect the varied architectural heritage of the city and affect the restoration of houses that were in varied stages of decay. It was also proposed that the 1855 courthouse be restored and become the core museum of a system that would encompass some of the Hill City's most significant structures. Richard Gifford, one of the executives at General Electric, was the prime mover in this effort. It became the major project of the Bicentennial Commission, which was formed to plan the city's celebration and recommend legacy projects which would enrich the future.

To finance the observance, the Bicentennial Commission struck a commemorative medal in silver and bronze. The obverse bore two figures, a man and a woman, representing the city's Quaker founders, and the reverse featured the front elevation of the courthouse. Lynchburg Foundry cast a small replica of the courthouse and donated this popular souvenir bank as its gift to the celebration. Both souvenirs were offered to the public during the 1975 holiday season, and sales were brisk.

"The Glorious Fourth" was celebrated, despite the threat of rain, by the entire population. Although there were a few who grumbled, all of the merchants in town were encouraged to briefly close and give their employees the chance to observe the day in proper fashion. The center of festivities was Miller Park, and for the first time citizens from every race and ethnic background celebrated the birth of their country together. Many former residents returned to Lynchburg to observe the day with family, friends, and neighbors. A separate commemoration was also held on Liberty Mountain, the new home of Liberty Baptist College.

There was a huge parade, a rededication of the restored Fireman's Fountain in Miller Park, an exhibit at the Fine Arts Center featuring the work of local artists, sporting events for every taste at a number of venues, a craft show, bus tours of the historic sections of the city, a photography show that chronicled the area's history from the invention of the daguerreotype to 1976, dedication of the Courthouse Museum, musical performances chronicling 200 years of American music, and a fireworks display that drew thousands. Even the 1936 gala Sesqui-centennial celebration paled in comparison with this citywide event; however, it proved to be but a rehearsal for Lynchburg's own bicentennial a decade later.

One of Lynchburg's "birthday gifts" to its citizens was a new high school. Sited on the western edge of the city, Heritage High School was described by some as a "peace offering" to those families that had been annexed against their wishes. During the 1976–1977 session, the new school occupied the campus of Sandusky Middle School, and then in the fall of 1977 the faculty and student body moved into the new building. Very quickly it became a spirited rival to E.C. Glass, and the healthy competition has grown over the years, serving to strengthen the academic and athletic reputations of both institutions.

CHAPTER TEN

BEGIN THE JUBILEE

1977–2007

Anne Spencer, perhaps Lynchburg's most celebrated published poet, died on July 26, 1975, at the age of 93, and within a year her home and studio, "Edankraal," were nominated as state and national landmarks. On February 26, 1977, they were dedicated in a moving ceremony attended by family, friends, and dignitaries representing the city and the state. This posthumous recognition of this remarkable representative of the Harlem Renaissance was also an acknowledgment of the role she played in the cultural history of her adopted city.

On the centennial of her birth in February 1982, she was accorded further homage by the local media that would have both pleased and bemused her. One of the featured speakers that day was Yolanda King, the daughter of the late Dr. Martin Luther King Jr. The contrast between the event Ms. King took part in, and that which had brought her father to Lynchburg, is significant. In 1962 the battle for civil rights still hung in the balance, and the audience at E.C. Glass was preparing for a long struggle. Twenty years later citizens gathered, regardless of race, to celebrate poetic genius and creativity. At last, Anne Spencer was coming into her own and Lynchburg was coming of age.

For the next 20 years her son, Chauncey Spencer, shared his mother's legacy with the world. Before his own death in the summer of 2002, he saw her beloved garden bloom again and her portrait grace the obverse of a commemorative medal struck to honor her during Lynchburg's 1986 bicentennial celebration. Chauncey Spencer was worthy of recognition in his own right. In the years before World War II his efforts of behalf of black pilots paved the way for the Tuskegee Airmen. His exploits and those of his comrades won the admiration and support of the then senator from Missouri, Harry S Truman. Together they worked to gain admittance for young men from black colleges and universities into the Civilian Pilot Training Program, and eventually into the Army Air Corps.

One of the most popular ideas developed by Lynchburgers as part of the nation's bicentennial was Kaleidoscope. Beginning in 1975, it has evolved as the central event marking the transition from summer to fall in the Hill City. Commencing with "Day in the Park," a celebration for all ages, it moves to an art show where works by dozens of artists from all over the region are featured and offered for sale. It finally moves to the Virginia Ten Miler, considered by serious runners to be one of the ten best short road races in the United States. Over the years Kaleidoscope has included tours of local industries, a craft show, and an antique show. Like a child's kaleidoscope, it is constantly changing to reflect the interests of the citizens of Lynchburg. In 1986 it was combined with the city's birthday to create a party that never seemed to end.

In 1980 the favored Lynchburg shopping precinct shifted from Pittman Plaza to the new River Ridge Mall. Despite the conversion of the upper level of the Lynchburg Public Library in 1987 for the local history and genealogical collections of Jones Memorial Library, these efforts only briefly stemmed the inevitable decline of the city's first shopping center. It is ironic that Pittman Plaza, or "the Plaza" as it became known, began to lose its place in the city's business structure as downtown Lynchburg began to enjoy something of a revival.

It has often been said that Lynchburg is a great place to raise a family. Since 1980, when Westminster-Canterbury opened its doors, the city has become an ideal place for retirement. In the last 23 years, Westminster-Canterbury has been joined by Valley View and the Summit. There are also a number of smaller retirement homes as well as long-term care facilities in the area. Lynchburg is able to provide a number of activities senior citizens enjoy, including a varied offering of the arts, recreation for every ability, and access to the city's rich past.

Particularly popular with seniors, and in fact with every age, are the six historic districts that include architectural treasures from the late eighteenth to the early twentieth centuries. One of the most popular local "sports" is naming the Seven Hills of Lynchburg. Those most often cited are: Diamond, Courthouse, Garland, Federal, Daniels, White Rock, and Franklin. In 1985 the Piedmont District of the Blue Ridge Mountains Council of the Boy Scouts of America, with the help of a number of local citizens, inaugurated the ten-mile long "Lynchburg Heritage Trail." It is part of a national program of similar trails, and scouts who complete it receive a special medal featuring the 1855 courthouse.

By 2000, Courthouse, Daniel's, Diamond, Federal, and Garland had become well-established historic districts. House by house, street by street, and district by district buildings long neglected have been restored, not as museums filled with exhibits, but as homes. Every year during Historic Garden Week, Kaleidoscope, or at Christmas, some of these restored dwellings are opened to the public. Each time this happens, the foresight and hard work of those women and men who saw the possibilities contained in the concept of historic districts is affirmed. In 2003 Rivermont was added to the list of historic districts, and in October of that year the first "Historic Lynchburg Ghost Walk" was held there, between the Miller-Claytor House and Randolph-Macon Woman's College. Needless to say it was a success; Lynchburgers love the past, even the ethereal.

LYNCHBURG

The Friends of the Academy of Music Theatre had transferred ownership of the historic structure to Liberty University in 1985 with the understanding that it would be returned to them if the university did not restore the academy by 1990. Initially there was a flurry of activity on Main Street, but then it came to an abrupt halt, because it was necessary to divert the financial resources of the university to other uses, and so the theatre was essentially abandoned. In 1990, the arrangement between the Friends of the Academy and Liberty University was renewed for another five years. Then in 1993 Lynchburg was hit by what weather experts described as a "wind shear."

In addition to hundreds of trees being destroyed, the steeples of First Baptist Church and Court Street Baptist Church, and the rear of the Academy of Music Theatre were seriously damaged. The steeple of First Baptist toppled into the sanctuary requiring a major renovation. Although the steeple of Court Street Baptist Church was ruined, the fabric of the building remained intact. Both churches were repaired in a relatively short time. The academy was not so fortunate.

The damage to the theatre was more severe because the 1911 fire had actually weakened the structural supports of the stage house or fly tower. The storm had finished the devastation begun by the blaze. While removing the rear of the building was begun in a timely manner, the extensive damage done 82 years earlier was unknown and the tower collapsed, damaging the business behind it. All work stopped, and the academy was left open to the elements and the city's pigeon population until the following spring. In March 1994, Liberty University returned what was left of the building to the newly reorganized Academy of Music Theatre, Inc. At this point another serious effort was begun to save and restore this beaux-arts treasure.

An anonymous gift of $25,000 made it possible to close the rear of the building. Then in a series of carefully planned steps, the structural integrity of the academy was stabilized. When the Lynchburg Gas Company was purchased by Columbia Gas of Virginia, its downtown office was acquired by the academy's board of trustees. This structure, built on the site of the old Union Hotel and made famous by Lucy Minor Otey and her hospital, was a perfect home for the academy's educational programs. When the Price and Clements Building at the rear of the theatre became available, it too was purchased. Thus a disaster in 1993 worked to the advantage of "Virginia's premier historic theatre."

It was now possible to restore the original building and develop the other structures into an arts complex that would revitalize the upper end of Main Street. In the summer of 2003, the Academy of Music Theatre merged with the Lynchburg Fine Arts Center to form the Academy of Fine Arts, and property values in downtown began to rise in anticipation of the reopening of the Academy Theatre for its centennial in 2005. The Lynchburg City Council, which has been very supportive of urban renewal projects, in

October 2003 gave the Academy of Fine Arts $1.2 million to aid in completing the first phase of the construction of its Main Street complex.

In the decade between Lynchburg's two bicentennial celebrations, the city rediscovered its waterfront, and in a sense returned to the place of its birth. As railroads became less important in the late 1960s, local lines of track were abandoned and eventually removed, leaving an ugly scar across Lynchburg's center. However, the Friends of Lynchburg Stream Valleys, a group of dedicated citizens that included Ruskin Freer and Ed Page, worked to transform what appeared to be urban decay into a natural oasis in the midst of a modern city. The Blackwater Creek Natural Area was dedicated in 1979 and three years later became part of the prestigious National Recreational Trail System.

Dr. Freer, a descendant of Lynchburg's pioneer Quakers, taught biology at Lynchburg College for 40 years and was recognized nationally for his knowledge of the flora and fauna of the Blue Ridge Mountains. His carefully prepared design for the plantings of trees, shrubs, and wild flowers has over the last quarter of a century created the illusion that the Blackwater Creek Natural Area has always been there. Since 1979 many of the animals that once roamed the region that became Lynchburg have returned to this recreated wilderness area, particularly deer.

Bike paths and hiking trails allow the average citizen to escape the noise and confusion of the work-a-day world and cross Lynchburg without being conscious that the city even exists. In 2003, the Awareness Garden Foundation dedicated a memorial to those Lynchburgers whose lives have been affected by cancer. It is located at the entrance to the trail dedicated to the memory of Ed Page. When the last links in this ambitious design are completed, the revitalized riverfront will be united to the city's green heart.

The flood of the twentieth century occurred in Lynchburg in November 1985. Many industries on the banks of the James River were damaged, and floodwaters almost covered the arches of the Williams Viaduct. This disaster taught the city's planners that any new construction along the riverfront must be minimal and able to survive future inundations. The Ninth Street revitalization project, which began in 1996, incorporates this reality into its overall plan and is scheduled for completion in 2005. Some of the components are already in place.

No sooner had the nation's two-hundredth birthday been observed in traditional fashion than the citizens of the Hill City began to devote a great deal of energy to preparing for the bicentennial of Lynchburg's designation as a town by the Virginia General Assembly. The city had celebrated this anniversary twice, in 1886 and 1936, but the celebration in 1986 was intended to surpass them both—and it did.

One of the most persistent rumors related to the sesquicentennial celebration of 1936 was that a box of memorabilia associated with the event was stored somewhere in the city. Shortly after the city council established the Bicentennial Commission, the mysterious treasure trove was discovered in one of the city's storage facilities. It had been sealed on the last night of the 1936 celebration and when it was opened on September 29, 1983, only one item was missing. Someone had stolen the Sesquicentennial Half Dollar, but left its souvenir folder. There were a number of letters addressed to various constituencies in the city, but fortunately one could not be delivered. It was addressed to the "Colored Bicentennial Committee." By 1986, Lynchburg was becoming a fully integrated community where such designations were obsolete.

In the early nineteenth century, when tobacco determined the destiny of Lynchburg, shipping the golden leaf to Richmond often proved the most difficult task in the production process. Then the batteaux made their appearance on the river and the problem was solved. Soon the sleek flat bottom vessels were making their way to the capital, laden with central Virginia's cash crop. Not since the Dutch "flyboat" of the seventeenth century has a craft been so well suited to its purpose. The era of the batteaux was brief; the railroad was faster and cheaper, and soon the batteaux vanished.

Then in 1983, Joe Ayres, a nineteenth-century man trapped in the twentieth century, discovered the remains of a batteau in the ooze in the James River at Richmond. Ayres' dream of bringing back the batteaux was realized on May 30, 1986, when the first James River Batteaux Festival began close to the site of the Lynch ferry. Every year since this bicentennial event, the batteaux have raced from Lynchburg to Richmond, easily slipping from one century back into another for a few glorious days when time stands still.

The conclusion of the bicentennial celebration in October 1986 was a gala affair that ended with a gigantic birthday party at Lynchburg Stadium, which included a cake so large that it covered a flatbed truck! The city of Galway, Ireland, the birthplace of Charles Lynch, sent gifts and a representative to this celebration blessed with perfect weather. (There was never a formal relationship with Galway, but on July 4, 1996, Rueil-Malmaison, France, did officially become Lynchburg's first sister city.) There were actually two parades, one downtown on October 15, and a larger parade the following day, which commenced at E.C. Glass High School and ended at the stadium.

The festivities began on the morning of October 16, with the dedication of a plaque at the old courthouse. This event was sponsored by the Lynchburg Committee of the National Society of the Colonial Dames of America in the Commonwealth of Virginia. After unveiling their plaque, "Point of Beginning," which honored the founders of the city, noted architectural historian and Lynchburg native S. Allen Chambers delivered the dedicatory address. The parade began at 2 p.m.; the actual celebration started at 7 p.m., and the stands were packed.

Members of the Lynchburg Police Department ran a relay from Richmond to Lynchburg carrying a copy of the city's charter from the Governor Gerald Bailes, and they entered the stadium right on time to the cheers of the crowd. There were speeches by the governor and Mayor Jimmie Bryan, as well as tributes in honor of a host of Lynchburgers, past and present. There were songs and hymns, as well as band performances. Then an army of volunteers served birthday cake to everyone while the crowd sang the city's bicentennial song. Finally, the lights were extinguished and the Lynchburg Fire Department began a large-scale fireworks display. The festivities finally ended at 10 p.m. It was truly a night to remember, and a fitting climax to three years of work by the Bicentennial Commission's respective committees.

There were additional events celebrating the city's birthday until the end of the year. Joe Ayres and the Good Fortune Minstrels presented a musical program, *Boatmen, Fancy Goods, and River Rats—Tales and Legends of the Mighty James* at Lynchburg College on October 22. On November 9, Agudath Sholom Synagogue hosted a pictorial history of the congregation. The Woman's Club of Lynchburg presented *Don't Bother Your Pretty Little Head*, a light-hearted musical history of the club from its founding in 1903 until 1986. The new time capsule was sealed and placed in the downtown branch of the Lynchburg Public Library, so it would not be lost for 50 years like the box from the Sesquicentennial. The year ended as it had begun, with a New Years Eve celebration at the City Market.

In 1968, Lucy Harrison Miller Baber and Evelyn Lee Moore wrote *Behind the Old Brick Wall, A Cemetery Story*, preserving in print one of the city's most precious sites that seemed on the verge of vanishing. Opened to burials in 1806, the Old City Cemetery was integrated from the beginning, but by the nation's bicentennial many of its monuments seemed damaged beyond repair, while others had vanished into the weeds and brush. Only the Confederate section, lovingly tended since 1866 by the Southern Memorial Association, and containing the graves of 2,200 soldiers from 14 states, reminded citizens of what used to be Lynchburg's most famous burial ground. Then a miracle occurred thanks to the dedication of a group of preservationists led by Lucy Baber's daughter, Jane Baber White. The revitalized Southern Memorial Association has transformed the cemetery into a garden spot and one of the most popular tourist destinations in Lynchburg.

In 1987, the building that had been the office of Dr. John Jay Terrell was moved from Rock Castle Farm in Campbell County to a site next to the Confederate section of the Old City Cemetery. It was restored and divided into two areas: one represents Dr. Terrell's office as it might have been in the 1860s; the other is a recreation of a pest house room where he treated the victims of smallpox with the help of the Sisters of Charity.

Dr. Terrell was also responsible for controlling an outbreak of glanders, a disease destroying the horses and mules that were essential to the Confederate forces. His contribution in saving thousands of animals is commemorated by the Quartermaster's Glanders Stable Exhibit, which has been placed near the New Potter's Field. Every year this section of the cemetery, reserved for the indigent citizens of Lynchburg, is covered with a carpet of antique daffodils planted as Eagle Scout projects. The key to the revitalization of the cemetery has been the host volunteers recruited by Jane White.

The brush and briars have been banished and replaced by an exceptional collection of antique roses, medicinal herbs, and a lotus pond. The monuments have been salvaged, cleaned, and when possible repaired. An attractive entrance welcomes the visitor into a site that is on the National Register of Historic Places and the Virginia Landmarks Register. The construction of a cemetery center provides a home for the Southern Memorial Association, and the Lucy Baber Research Library for Cemetery Records, and the Tom Burford Horticultural Library. Modern technology now makes the nineteenth and twentieth centuries available to the modern scholar or student of genealogy.

Two more structures, the Hearse House and Caretakers' Museum and the Station House Museum have been added to the cemetery. The former houses a horse-drawn hearse once used by W.D. Diuguid, a vehicle made by Lynchburg's Thornhill Wagon Works, and a collection of tools that might have been used in the cemetery a century ago. The latter is actually the station that served Stapleton in Amherst County from 1898 until 1937. It captures a moment during World War I when one of Virginia's sons has returned home to be buried. It is a somber moment, but like everything associated with the Old City Cemetery, it brings life into focus.

The Woman's Club's major bicentennial project, the restoration of the dolphin fountain formerly placed at the base of Monument Terrace, was not officially dedicated until October 1987. Like the sesquicentennial box, the dolphin had languished in storage and required a year to be completely refurbished. It is now the centerpiece of "Batteaux Landing," the remodeled City Market.

Wherever one turns in Lynchburg there are reminders of the wars that have called forth the best in our citizens, and sometimes the worst. Just when it seemed that religious and ethnic prejudices were banished from the community, vandals painted a swastika on the front wall of Agudath Shalom Synagogue. The symbol of hatred was quickly removed, but the scar remained on the psyche of Lynchburg. In 1993 the Holocaust Education Foundation of Central Virginia was formed in partnership with the city schools to hopefully prevent this kind of desecration from occurring again. Beginning in middle school, students study the persecution of Jews and other minority groups by the Nazis in the belief that they will learn that toleration of diversity as well as rejection of prejudice have valuable lessons to teach. The first students to study the Holocaust are now in college, and hopefully the lessons they learned are being passed on to others who have never visited the Hill City.

The Junior League of Lynchburg unveiled its plan for a children's museum in 1992. The dilapidated J.W. Wood building on Ninth Street near the river was transformed into Amazement Square, and in 1998 the league sponsored its first Cultural Festival in the first multi-disciplinary hands-on children's museum in the commonwealth. By 2003, more than 200,000 visitors annually from all over the region have enjoyed the exhibits, activities, and programs that fill its four floors. Children's museums have become a vital part of the nation's educational landscape since the end of World War II, and Amazement Square was planned to take advantage of the successes and avoid the failures of earlier efforts. Absolutely state of the art, Amazement Square has become a mecca for adults and children.

Amazement Square forms one of the anchors at the base of Ninth Street; Riverviews Artspace is the other. In 1996 the private, non-profit organization began planning the renovation of the old Craddock-Terry Shoe Company warehouse. In 2002 the transformation of the building began. When it is completed there will be studio and living areas for artists, as well as another badly needed gallery and commercial space.

Across the street, and slightly above Amazement Square, the J.W. Ould Building has been converted into the new home of the Lynchburg Department of Human Services and the Division of Social Services. Completed in 2003, it is a perfect example of the revitalization of older structures for modern needs, and proof that a new spirit is transforming the Hill City into an attractive destination for tourists, new businesses, and new residents.

In the summer of 2003 the complete refurbishing of Monument Terrace began. Work on stabilizing Lynchburg's "signature" was long overdue, and coupled with the restoration of the 1855 courthouse, it will be completed in time for Virginia's Quadricentennial celebration in 2007. The Lynchburg Museum and its collections have been moved to temporary locations until the work is completed, but the number of visitors to the city's first museum continues to increase.

The Legacy Museum, dedicated to the study of African-American history in Lynchburg and central Virginia, opened in 2000. Located in the heart of the black community next to the Old City Cemetery, it has begun to assemble a collection of artifacts and sources—both written and oral—that will preserve the history of a long neglected segment of the community and share it with all of Lynchburg's citizens. It has already proven a particularly valuable resource for teachers in the city schools.

LYNCHBURG

Tennis has been a passion, almost an obsession with some Lynchburgers, but few of the players at Oakwood or Boonsboro Country Clubs were aware at mid-century that in the inner city Dr. Walter Johnson was training world champions who would transform the game once reserved for royalty. Dr. Johnson, Arthur Ashe, and Althea Gibson are gone now, but their legacy will last as long as youngsters believe that they can reach the court at Wimbledon through hard work and dedication, without regard to their gender or the color of their skin. The Legacy Museum can help keep those dreams alive by reminding us all of the path we have traveled as a city, and of those who have blazed the trail before us.

In the last quarter of the twentieth century Lynchburg's African-American community produced a circle of leaders who served not only the members of their own race, but the city at large. Men and women like Edward Barksdale, Vivian Camm, Gilliam Cobbs, Yvonne Ferguson, Junius Haskins, Edna Holmes, Carl Hutcherson Jr., Arelia S. Langhorne, Pauline Fletcher Maloney, Haywood Robinson, M.W. Thornhill Jr., and Anne R. Wesley have helped to bring closer the full realization of a society of equals envisioned by the Quakers who laid the foundations of Lynchburg.

The Johnson Health Center opened at 320 Federal Street in 1999 on the site of Lynchburg's last tobacco factory that burned a number of years ago. Along with Daily Bread, Churches for Urban Ministry, and the Free Clinic of Central Virginia, it offers help to those citizens who a century ago might have been forgotten or ignored. There is a wonderful irony in the fact that the descendants of men and women who labored for subsistence wages in the tobacco industry are receiving health care on the site of one of those factories.

In December 2000, the Historic Sandusky Foundation, Inc., was established to convert Charles Johnson's mansion into a house museum preserving the moment when retired Major Edward Hutter played the reluctant host to General David Hunter and his staff on the eve of the Battle of Lynchburg. Dr. Peter Houck, whose work with the Monacan helped them gain official recognition from the Virginia General Assembly, spearheaded the movement to purchase and restore this property, which is a Virginia Historic Landmark and is listed on the National Register of Historic Places. Nationally recognized Civil War historian James "Bud" Robertson Jr., has narrated an audio driving tour of Lynchburg's Civil War sites, with the Union Headquarters at Sandusky as the first stop.

The Academy of Fine Arts provides the anchor for the upper end of Main Street, while the Bluff Walk Center will provide a base for the lower end of Lynchburg's main thoroughfare. Situated in an old warehouse, the Craddock Terry Hotel and its Shoemaker's Restaurant, Packet's Restaurant, and Brew Pub overlooks the waterfront;

a perfect location to bring tourists and local residents back to the river where the city was born. Behind this movement is the dynamic leadership of Lynch's Landing, a non-profit volunteer organization dedicated to restoring downtown as the focus of city life. The decay that began in 1960 has definitely been reversed.

Sometimes the present seems to intrude into the past. In October 2002, two juveniles, driving far beyond the speed limit to avoid the police, destroyed the obelisk at Fort Early that honored Jubal A. Early, the Confederate general who saved Lynchburg from General Hunter in June 1864. The boys survived the crash, but they caused a commotion. Some wish to replace the monument, while others would prefer that it remain permanently removed. With the support of the city government, the monument will be replaced; the past must not be edited lest truth be placed in jeopardy.

Another example of an anniversary intruding upon the sensibilities of the present occurred in February 2003, when the Lewis and Clark Corps of Discovery II visited Lynchburg. It was the second stop on a nationwide tour that would mark the route of the exploration of the Louisiana Territory 200 years ago. Lewis and Clark opened up the West to exploration and exploitation, and Clark's support of black slavery was typical of his class and time. The organizers of this travelling exhibit are to be commended for their honesty in dealing with a host of sensitive subjects and seeking the help of local experts to place the Corps of Discovery in its proper historic and local context. The visit was a complete success, and despite the snow and mud, the lecture tent was filled for every event with young and old eager to learn more about this pivotal event in American history. The study of the past should be based not on fantasies and myths, but on facts—even those that may at times make us uncomfortable.

One of the problems, which face Lynchburg's citizens in the twenty-first century, is how to preserve the best of the past as a legacy for the future without sacrificing truth. From its beginning, Lynchburg has been part of the wider world; it has never existed in isolation. Events that could not be controlled have altered the course of our history, and in turn Lynchburg's sons and daughters have changed the unfolding of circumstances that have influenced the destiny of the region, state, nation, and yes, even the world.

Anne Royall deplored the number of houses of worship in Lynchburg in the early nineteenth century; now "the City of Churches" counts over 200 within its limits. Perhaps in the last analysis, Lynchburg's future lies with them, Lynchburg's colleges, its schools, its museums, and the strength of its citizens.

BIBLIOGRAPHY

Baber, Lucy Harrison Miller and Evelyn Lee Moore. *Behind the Old Brick Wall, A Cemetery Story*. Lynchburg, VA: Lynchburg Committee of the National Society of Colonial Dames of America, 1968.

Bedford City County Museum. *Bedford's Images Old and New*. Bedford, VA, 2004.

Bell, James Pinkney; *Our Quaker Friends of Ye Olden Time*. Lynchburg, VA: J.C. Bell, 1905.

Bratton, Mary Elizabeth Kinnier. *Our Goodly Heritage A History of the First Presbyterian Church of Lynchburg Virginia, 1815–1940*. Lynchburg, VA: J.P. Bell Company, Inc., 1940.

Breen, T.H. and Stephen Innes. *Myne Owne Ground; Race and Freedom on Virginia's Eastern Shore, 1640–1676*. New York, NY: Oxford University Press, 1980.

Brown, Douglas Summers. *Lynchburg's Pioneer Quakers and Their Meeting House*. Lynchburg, VA: Warwick House, 1997.

Burford, Iva Campbell. *Now the Song, Memories of a Childhood Spent in Lynchburg's Miller Orphanage During the 1920s*. Lynchburg, VA: Warwick House, 2001.

Cabell, Margaret Anthony. *Sketches and Recollections of Lynchburg by the Oldest Inhabitant (1858)*. Lynchburg, VA: Lynchburg Historical Foundation, 1974.

Chambers, S. Allen, Jr. *Lynchburg: An Architectural History*. Charlottesville, VA: University Press of Virginia, 1981.

Childs, Benjamin Guy. *The Negroes of Lynchburg, Virginia*. Charlottesville, VA: Surber-Arundale Company, 1923.

Christian, W. Ashby. *Lynchburg and Its People*. Lynchburg, VA: J.P. Bell, 1900.

Cole, Jeffrey S. "The impact of the Great Depression and New Deal on the urban South: Lynchburg, Virginia as a case study, 1929–1941." Ph.D. dissertation. Bowling Green State University, 1998.

Cook, Samuel. *Monacans and Miners: Native American and Coal Mining Communities in Appalachia*. Lincoln, NE: University of Nebraska Press, 2000.

Cornelius, Roberta D. *The History of Randolph-Macon Woman's College*. Chapel Hill, NC: University of North Carolina Press, 1951.

Bibliography

Cox, Harold E. Hill City Trolleys: *Street Railways of Lynchburg, Va.* Forty Fort, PA: published by author, 1977.

Craddock, Martha Helen Cleveland. *The Streets of Lynchburg.* Lynchburg, VA: H.E. Howard, Inc., 1986.

Craighill, Edley, *The Musketeers.* Lynchburg, VA: J.P. Bell, 1931.

Delaney, Ted and Phillip Wayne Rhodes. *Free Blacks of Lynchburg, Virginia, 1805–1865.* Lynchburg, VA: Warwick House, 2001.

Derks, Scott, ed. *The Value of A Dollar, Prices and Incomes in the United States, 1860–1999.* Millerton, NY: Grey House Publishing, 1999.

Dunn, William R. and T. Gibson Hobbs, Jr. *Historical Sketches from The Iron Worker.* Lynchburg, VA: The Lynchburg Historical Foundation, 1984.

Elson, James M. *Academy of Music, Lynchburg, Virginia: The Golden Age of Live Performance.* Lynchburg, VA: The Lynchburg Historical Foundation, 1993.

Ferguson, Harry S. "The Participation of the Lynchburg, Virginia Negro in Politics, 1865–1900," unpublished M.A. thesis, Virginia State College, 1954.

Frischkorn, Rebecca T. and Reuben M. Rainey. *Half My World: The Garden of Anne Spencer, A History and Guide.* Lynchburg, VA: Warwick House Publishing, 2003.

Helper, Hinton A. *Centennial Souvenir of Lynchburg, Virginia.* New York, NY: South Publishing Company, reprint: Lynchburg, VA: North Buckley, 1986.

Horner, John V. and P.B. Winfree, Jr., eds. *The Saga of a City: Lynchburg, Virginia.* Lynchburg, VA: Lynchburg Sesqui-Centennial Association, 1936.

Houck, Peter W. *Indian Island in Amherst County.* Lynchburg: Warwick House, 1984.

———. *A Prototype of a Confederate Hospital Center in Lynchburg, Virginia.* Lynchburg, VA: Warwick House, 1986.

———., ed. *Tour Lynchburg A Personal Tour Guide to Lynchburg, Virginia.* Lynchburg, VA: Sarah Winston Henry Branch of the Association for the Preservation of Virginia Antiquities, 1985.

Jefferson, Thomas. *Notes on the State of Virginia.* ed. William Peden. Chapel Hill, NC: University of North Carolina Press, 1955.

Langhorne, Orra. *Southern Sketches from Virginia: 1881–1901.* Ed. Charles E. Wynes. Charlottesville, VA: University Press of Virginia, 1964.

Laurant, Darrell. *A City Unto Itself, Lynchburg, Virginia in the 20th Century.* Lynchburg, VA: The News and Advance, 1997.

Lynch's Ferry: A Journal of Local History. Lynchburg, VA: Warwick House. Various articles.

McCary, Ben C. *Indians in Seventeenth Century Virginia.* Williamsburg, VA: Virginia 350th Celebration Corporation, 1957.

LYNCHBURG

McCray, Carrie Allen. *Freedom's Child: The Story of My Mother, a Confederate General's Black Daughter.* Chapel Hill, NC: Algonquin Books, 1998.

Memoirs of Life In and Out of the Army in Virginia During the War Between the States. Comp. Susan Leigh Blackford, ed. and annotated Charles Minor Blackford. Two volumes. Lynchburg, VA: J.P. Bell, 1894. Revised ed. and foreword by Peter W. Houck. Lynchburg, VA: Warwick House, 1996.

Morgan, Edmund S. *American Slavery/American Freedom: The Ordeal of Colonial Virginia.* New York, NY: W.W. Norton, 1975.

Morris, George and Susan Foutz. *Lynchburg in the Civil War: The City—The People—The Battle.* Lynchburg, VA: H.E. Howard, 1984.

Percy, Alfred. *The Amherst County Story.* Madison Heights, VA: Percy Press, 1961.

Potter, Clifton, ed. *Jubilee: A History of Lynchburg College.* Lynchburg, VA: Lynchburg College, 1978.

Potter, Dorothy T. and Clifton W. Potter, Jr. *Lynchburg. . . "The most interesting Spot. . .".* Lynchburg, VA: Beric Press, 1985.

Potter, Edmund. "Westover: The Changing Functions of a Resort Structure," M.A. thesis, Charlottesville, VA: the University of Virginia, 1995.

Rountree, Helen. *Pocahantas's People: The Powhatan Indians of Virginia Through Four Centuries.* Norman, OK: University of Oklahoma Press, 1996.

————. *The Powhatan Indians of Virginia: Their Traditional Culture.* Norman, OK: University of Oklahoma Press, 1898.

Salmon, Nina V., ed. *Anne Spencer: "Ah how poets sing and die!"* Lynchburg, VA: Warwick House Publishing, 2001.

Schewel, Michael J. "Local Politics in Lynchburg, Virginia in the 1880s," *The Virginia Magazine of History and Biography,* vol. 89, no. 2, April 1981, 170–180.

Scruggs, Philip Lightfoot. *The History of Lynchburg, Virginia: 1786–1946.* Lynchburg: J. P. Bell, 1971.

Sketchbook of Lynchburg, Va., Its People and Its Trade. reprint of the 1887 edition. Lynchburg, VA: Hillcrest Associates, 1987.

Smith, John. *The Complete Works of Captain John Smith*, ed. by Philip L. Barbour. Chapel Hill, NC: University of North Carolina, 1986.

Stories of the Stones, Interpretive Plaques in the Old City Cemetery. Lynchburg, VA: The Southern Memorial Association, 1999.

Tripp, Steven Elliott. *Yankee Town, Southern City: Race and Class Relations in Civil War Lynchburg.* New York, NY: New York University Press, 1996.

Wake, Orville W. "The First Fifty Years: A History of Lynchburg College, 1903–1953." Ph.D. dissertation, Charlottesville, VA: University of Virginia, 1957.

Wiley, Lib. *Alongside the River, A History of Lynchburg's Congregations.* Lynchburg, VA: Bicentennial Commission, 1986.

Williams, Samuel. *A Brief History of Miller Home, Lynchburg Female Orphan Asylum.* Lynchburg, VA: J.P. Bell Company, Inc., 1964.

Worrall, Jay Jr. *The Friendly Virginians: America's First Quakers.* Athens, GA: Iberian Publishing, 1994.

INDEX

Index